MODERN POETS IN FOCUS: 1

MODERN POETS IN FOCUS

Each volume in this series features the poems of six poets with introductions to their work by the editor. Some of the poems have not been previously published in book form. Where possible, comments by the poets on their own work have been included. Each book focuses on: 1. A modern master who continues to influence those now writing in the English language; 2. A living poet celebrated on both sides of the Atlantic; 3. A poet's poet who has been somewhat neglected by the reading public; 4. A poet who has recently died but whose work is very much alive; 5. A new young poet whose reputation has already begun to grow; 6. A poet never before published in book form by a London-based commercial publisher.

Volume 1 (ed. Dannie Abse)
Edward Thomas, Ted Hughes, David Wright, Sidney Keyes, Douglas Dunn, Herbert Williams.
Volume 2 (ed. Jeremy Robson)
Wilfred Owen, Philip Larkin, Thomas Blackburn, Keith Douglas, Seamus Heaney, William Meredith.
Volume 3 (ed. Dannie Abse)
D.H. Lawrence, Robert Graves, Alastair Reid, Alun Lewis, Stewart Conn, Dabney Stuart.
Volume 4 (ed. Jeremy Robson)
Thomas Hardy, Dannie Abse, Vernon Scannell, Stevie Smith, Tony Harrison, Daniel Hoffman.
Volume 5 (ed. Dannie Abse)
Ezra Pound, Thom Gunn, Bernard Spencer, Sylvia Plath, Fleur Adcock, John Ormond.

MODERN POETS IN FOCUS: 1

Edited by

DANNIE ABSE

THE WOBURN PRESS : LONDON

This edition first published in 1973 by
WOBURN BOOKS LIMITED
67 Great Russell Street
London WC1B 3BT

First published by Corgi Books in 1971

Introduction and selection © Dannie Abse, 1971

ISBN 0 7130 0077 5

Acknowledgements for the use of copyright material will
be found on page 8 which is hereby made part of this
copyright page.

Printed in Great Britain by
Lewis Reprints Ltd.
member of Brown Knight & Truscott Group
London and Tonbridge

14. SEP. 1973

Contents

Acknowledgments

For permission to reproduce copyright material acknowledgments are owed to Ted Hughes for Crow Hears Fate Knock on the Door, The Contender, Existential Song, Song against the White Owl, and to Faber and Faber Ltd. for Wind, Witches, Hawk Roosting, View of a Pig, Cadenza and Crow Tyrannosaurus; to David Wright for Swift and Rook, to A. D. Peters Ltd. for poems from Moral Stories (André Deutsch), Monologue of a Deaf Man (André Deutsch), Adam at Evening (Hodder and Stoughton), and Nerve Ends (Hodder and Stoughton); to Routledge and Sons Ltd. for the poems by Sidney Keyes from his Collected Poems; to Douglas Dunn for After the War, Under the Stone, The Friendship of Young Poets and Backwaters, and to Faber and Faber Ltd. for The Patricians, Young Women in Rollers, Incident in the Shop, The Worst of all Loves, A Dream of Random Love and A Poem in Praise of the British; to the author for the poems by Herbert Williams. The two short prose pieces by Ted Hughes were taken from Poetry in the Making (Faber) and from The London Magazine (Ed. Alan Ross). The prose statements by David Wright, Douglas Dunn and Herbert Williams, were written especially for this volume.

EDWARD THOMAS

EDWARD THOMAS

No poet can write poems as if he were the first poet that ever existed. He has to be aware of his significant predecessors, he has to know what has been done and what can no longer be done. In 1936, Michael Roberts edited *The Faber Book of Modern Verse* and included those poets whom he felt had made notable developments in poetry technique, who were, in his view, innovators. He included only poems that seemed 'to add to the resources of poetry, to be likely to influence the future development of poetry and language'. His anthology included such poets as Gerard Manley Hopkins, W. B. Yeats, Ezra Pound, T. S. Eliot, D. H. Lawrence, Isaac Rosenberg, Wilfred Owen, W. H. Auden, and Dylan Thomas. Many young poets today will acknowledge their debt to such contributors of *The Faber Book of Modern Verse*.

Surprisingly, though, two other poets not in Michael Roberts' anthology, two country poets, Thomas Hardy and Edward Thomas would also be acknowledged by many English poets as being among those who have influenced them, and to whom they feel indebted. Moreoever, while the general reading public know and accept Hardy's work, the poems of Edward Thomas still remain unread by too many, and in the U.S.A. he is remembered, if at all, rather as a friend of Robert Frost than for being a poet in his own right.

Michael Roberts never included Edward Thomas in his anthology because he would have thought of him as a Georgian poet and by 1936 the very word 'Georgian' had become a term of critical abuse. Georgian country poetry was that school of verse which thrived during the years 1910–1925. Its patent faults were triviality of theme and sentimentality of expression. James Reeves has justly commented on the pedestrian tendency of most Georgian poetry, 'a tendency which too often leads to triviality, complacency, and the avoidance of strong personal feelings. It is possible to jog through volume after volume of Georgian lyrics without being in any way stirred to applause or to protest'.

Like other Georgian poets, Edward Thomas wrote about the English countryside but with such a strong personal feeling that the reader cannot but help experience the assault of genuine poetry. It is in no way possible to jog through Edward Thomas's poems without being stirred. His work is not complacent, it is not like so many Georgian lyrics, escape-verse. On the contrary, his poetry is an exposure of himself in which he displays not only his deep love of the English countryside but his suffering, his pessimism, his melancholy. These black moods of his had hardly anything to do with the fact that he was a soldier in the first World War, though as a soldier-poet perhaps he did have premonitions that he was destined to be killed in the trenches like Isaac Rosenberg and Wilfred Owen.

> Rain, midnight rain, nothing but the wild rain
> On this bleak hut, and solitude, and me
> Remembering again that I shall die
> And neither hear the rain nor give it thanks
> For washing me cleaner than I have been
> Since I was born into this solitude.

Even when this rather Keatsian melancholy spilled over into morbidity the music of his poems derived from no mechanical Georgian metronome. The reader can always hear the timbre of the real voice, the voice of a singular human being, the quirks of expression, the repetition of words so common in hesitant, conversational speech. What should be remembered too, was that Edward Thomas was not only a country poet but also a war poet. Indeed he began to write poetry only in 1915 at the mature age of 37. In the next two years, the last two years of his life, astonishingly he wrote over a hundred poems, a number of which quite naturally refer to the war situation directly and usually without the veneer of fashionable sentiment:

> I hate not Germans, nor grow hot
> With love of Englishmen, to please newspapers.
> Beside my hate for one fat patriot
> My hatred of the Kaiser is love true:
> A kind of god he is, banging a gong.

Like Owen and like Rosenberg, Edward Thomas could be very bitter about war and the ravages of war:

> Time swims before me, making as a day
> A thousand years, while the broad ploughland oak
> Roars mill-like and men strike and bear the stroke
> Of war as ever, audacious or resigned,
> And God still sits aloft in the array
> That we have wrought him, stone-deaf and stone-blind.

Yet at this mature age Edward Thomas did not have to join the army. Nobody was pressing him to do so. With his conscious anti-heroic attitude about war, his dislike of 'fat patriots' why did he join the doomed hordes in the trenches? Once a close friend of his, the novelist Eleanor Farjeon, asked him what he was fighting for. 'He stopped,' Miss Farjeon writes, 'and picked up a pinch of earth. "Literally for this." He crumbled it between finger and thumb and let it fall.'

Edward Thomas probably intended no morbid ambiguity in that gesture. His love of the English countryside, the English soil, is not only manifest in his poetry but also in the thirty hack books of prose that he had written over a score of years. Unpleasant as it may be to say it, war provided for Thomas some solution of his personal ills and conflicts. We know how he had laboured at work he did not enjoy and which had provided him with only a meagre living. We may guess that he did not or could not love his wife, Helen, wholeheartedly. Poems such as 'And you, Helen', and 'No One So Much As You' are beautifully but cruelly honest. Again, though he was a *questing* man, 'a man in search of his soul, he did not believe in, or gain solace from, any political or religious orthodoxy. 'The more one reflects on those twenty years of slavery as a self-employed hack', writes Dan Jacobson, 'on the miseries of self-thwarted creativity represented by those thirty books of prose, the more one is compelled to feel the outbreak of the war stabilized Thomas, and enabled him finally to find his own voice, by creating a kind of objective correlative, so to speak, for all that was most self-destructive within him. Far beneath the level of his wish or awareness, one suspects, he must have felt a certain relief at seeing the disharmonies which had made so much of his life an 'evil dream' were not his alone; at the realization that fears and despairs which for him had been purely psychic, so many states of mind, nothing else, and all the more solitary and shameful for being so, were now made manifest in the world at large, and that the forms they had taken were far more hideous than any he could ever have imagined. To put it more crudely still: even the directly suicidal impulses he had from time to time been afflicted with were now given some kind of external direction or sanction.'

The objective correlatives of his constitutional melancholy and pessimism were not expressed though in trench-poems with their landscapes of mud and blood and human desolations; rather they found expression in the darker aspect of eternal nature, as she is sometimes perceived on chilling occasions. Such is the poem, 'Owl' where Edward Thomas refers back to and contradicts Shakespeare's 'merry note'.

All of the night was quite barred out except
An owl's cry, a most melancholy cry.

Shaken out long and clear upon the hill,
No merry note, nor cause of merriment
But one telling me plain what I escaped
And others could not, that night, as in I went.

And salted was my food and my repose.
Salted and sobered too, by the bird's voice
Speaking for all who lay under the stars,
Soldiers and poor, unable to rejoice.

In 1917 Edward Thomas was killed at Arras. It was only after his death that his poems were collected. When he was alive his poems had been rejected by editors and even his friends did not recognize their true power and value. It was not until 1920 that his *Collected Poems* appeared. Now, more than fifty years later, as Vernon Scannell asserts, 'We should be grateful for the image he has left us of his world, that place where melancholy and muted gaiety are inextricably mixed, a place peopled by characters half real, half mythical, who are never still, always passing out of the poet's orbit; a place where a fresh wind of irony blows away the maudlin and the false. The reader who finds that he is barred from entering this world because of his training, prejudices, and preconceptions concerning the nature of poetry, would do well to re-think the principles on which his judgments are based, and the reader who is barred by defects of sensibility and imagination must accept the fact that he is deaf and blind to the work of one of the best of England's minor poets.'

WOMEN HE LIKED

Women he liked, did shovel-bearded Bob,
Old Farmer Hayward of the Heath, but he
Loved horses. He himself was like a cob,
And leather-coloured. Also he loved a tree.

For the life in them he loved most living things,
But a tree chiefly. All along the lane
He planted elms where now the stormcock sings
That travellers hear from the slow-climbing train.

Till then the track had never had a name
For all its thicket and the nightingales
That should have earned it. No one was to blame.
To name a thing beloved man sometimes fails.

Many years since, Bob Hayward died, and now
None passes there because the mist and the rain
Out of the elms have turned the lane to slough
And gloom, the name alone survives, Bob's Lane.

OLD MAN

Old Man, or Lad's-love, – in the name there's nothing
To one that knows not Lad's-love, or Old Man,
The hoar-green feathery herb, almost a tree,
Growing with rosemary and lavender.
Even to one that knows it well, the names
Half decorate, half perplex, the thing it is:
At least, what that is clings not to the names
In spite of time. And yet I like the names.

The herb itself I like not, but for certain
I love it, as some day the child will love it
Who plucks a feather from the door-side bush
Whenever she goes in or out of the house.
Often she waits there, snipping the tips and shrivelling
The shreds at last on to the path, perhaps
Thinking, perhaps of nothing, till she sniffs
Her fingers and runs off. The bush is still
But half as tall as she, though it is as old;
So well she clips it. Not a word she says;
And I can only wonder how much hereafter
She will remember, with that bitter scent,
Of garden rows, and ancient damson trees
Topping a hedge, a bent path to a door,
A low thick bush beside the door, and me
Forbidding her to pick.

                    As for myself,
Where first I met the bitter scent is lost.
I, too, often shrivel the grey shreds,
Sniff them and think and sniff again and try

Once more to think what it is I am remembering,
Always in vain. I cannot like the scent,
Yet I would rather give up others more sweet,
With no meaning, than this bitter one.

I have mislaid the key. I sniff the spray
And think of nothing; I see and I hear nothing;
Yet seem, too, to be listening, lying in wait
For what I should, yet never can, remember:
No garden appears, no path, no hoar-green bush
Of Lad's-love, or Old Man, no child beside,
Neither father nor mother, nor any playmate;
Only an avenue, dark, nameless, without end.

THE NEW HOUSE

Now first, as I shut the door,
   I was alone
In the new house; and the wind
   Began to moan.

Old at once was the house,
   And I was old;
My ears were teased with the dread
   Of what I was foretold,

Nights of storm, days of mist, without end;
   Sad days when the sun
Shone in vain: old griefs and griefs
   Not yet begun.

All was foretold me; naught
   Could I foresee;
But I learned how the wind would sound
   After these things should be.

THE OWL

Downhill I came, hungry, and yet not starved;
Cold, yet had heat within me that was proof
Against the North wind; tired, yet so that rest
Had seemed the sweetest thing under a roof.

Then at the inn I had food, fire, and rest,
Knowing how hungry, cold, and tired was I.
All of the night was quite barred out except
An owl's cry, a most melancholy cry.

Shaken out long and clear upon the hill,
No merry note, nor cause of merriment,
But one telling me plain what I escaped
And others could not, that night, as in I went.

And salted was my food, and my repose,
Salted and sobered, too, by the bird's voice
Speaking for all who lay under the stars,
Soldiers and poor, unable to rejoice.

WHAT SHALL I GIVE?

What shall I give my daughter the younger
More than will keep her from cold and hunger?
I shall not give her anything.
If she shared South Weald and Havering,
Their acres, the two brooks running between,
Paine's Brook and Weald Brook,
With pewit, woodpecker, swan, and rook,
She would be no richer than the queen
Who once on a time sat in Havering Bower
Alone, with the shadows, pleasure and power.
She could do no more with Samarkand,
Or the mountains of a mountain land
And its far white house above cottages
Like Venus above the Pleiades.
Her small hands I would not cumber
With so many acres and their lumber,
But leave her Steep and her own world
And her spectacled self with hair uncurled,
Wanting a thousand little things
That time without contentment brings.

AND YOU, HELEN

And you, Helen, what should I give you?
So many things I would give you
Had I an infinite great store
Offered me and I stood before
To choose. I would give you youth,
All kinds of loveliness and truth,
A clear eye as good as mine,
Lands, waters, flowers, wine,
As many children as your heart
Might wish for, a far better art
Than mine can be, all you have lost
Upon the travelling waters tossed,
Or given to me. If I could choose
Freely in that great treasure-house
Anything from any shelf,
I would give you back yourself,
And power to discriminate
What you want and want it not too late,
Many fair days free from care
And heart to enjoy both foul and fair,
And myself, too, if I could find
Where it lay hidden and it proved kind.

NO ONE SO MUCH AS YOU

No one so much as you
Loves this my clay,
Or would lament as you
Its dying day.

You know me through and through
Though I have not told,
And though with what you know
You are not bold.

None ever was so fair
As I thought you:
Not a word can I bear
Spoken against you.

All that I ever did
For you seemed coarse
Compared with what I hid
Nor put in force.

My eyes scarce dare meet you
Lest they should prove
I but respond to you
And do not love.

We look and understand,
We cannot speak
Except in trifles and
Words the most weak.

For I at most accept
Your love, regretting
That is all: I have kept
Only a fretting

That I could not return
All that you gave
And could not ever burn
With the love you have,

Till sometimes it did seem
Better it were
Never to see you more
Than linger here

With only gratitude
Instead of love –
A pine in solitude
Cradling a dove.

THE UNKNOWN BIRD

Three lovely notes he whistled, too soft to be heard
If others sang; but others never sang
In the great beech-wood all that May and June.
No one saw him: I alone could hear him
Though many listened. Was it but four years
Ago? or five? He never came again.

Oftenest when I heard him I was alone,
Nor could I ever make another hear.
La-la-la! he called, seeming far-off –
As if a cock crowed past the edge of the world,
As if the bird or I were in a dream.
Yet that he travelled through the trees and sometimes
Neared me, was plain, though somehow distant still
He sounded. All the proof is – I told men
What I had heard.

                    I never knew a voice,
Man, beast, or bird, better than this. I told
The naturalists; but neither had they heard
Anything like the notes that did so haunt me,
I had them clear by heart and have them still.
Four years, or five, have made no difference. Then
As now that La-la-la! was bodiless sweet:
Sad more than joyful it was, if I must say
That it was one or other, but if sad
'Twas sad only with joy too, too far off
For me to taste it. But I cannot tell
If truly never anything but fair
The days were when he sang, as now they seem.

This surely I know, that I who listened then,
Happy sometimes, sometimes suffering
A heavy body and a heavy heart,
Now straightway, if I think of it, become
Light as that bird wandering beyond my shore.

A PRIVATE

This ploughman dead in battle slept out of doors
Many a frozen night, and merrily
Answered staid drinkers, good bedmen, and all bores:
'At Mrs. Greenland's Hawthorn Bush', said he,
'I slept.' None knew which bush. Above the town,
Beyond 'The Drover', a hundred spot the down
In Wiltshire. And where now at last he sleeps
More sound in France – that, too, he secret keeps.

CELANDINE

Thinking of her had saddened me at first,
Until I saw the sun on the celandines lie
Redoubled, and she stood up like a flame,
A living thing, not what before I nursed,
The shadow I was growing to love almost,
The phantom, not the creature with bright eye
That I had thought never to see, once lost.

She found the celandines of February
Always before us all. Her nature and name
Were like those flowers, and now immediately
For a short swift eternity back she came,
Beautiful, happy, simply as when she wore
Her brightest bloom among the winter hues
Of all the world; and I was happy too,
Seeing the blossoms and the maiden who
Had seen them with me Februarys before,
Bending to them as in and out she trod
And laughed, with locks sweeping the mossy sod.

But this was a dream: the flowers were not true,
Until I stooped to pluck from the grass there
One of five petals and I smelt the juice
Which made me sigh, remembering she was no
    more,
Gone like a never perfectly recalled air.

RAIN

Rain, midnight rain, nothing but the wild rain
On this bleak hut, and solitude, and me
Remembering again that I shall die
And neither hear the rain nor give it thanks
For washing me cleaner than I have been
Since I was born into this solitude.
Blessed are the dead that the rain rains upon:
But here I pray that none whom once I loved
Is dying tonight or lying still awake
Solitary, listening to the rain,
Either in pain or thus in sympathy
Helpless among the living and the dead,
Like a cold water among broken reeds,
Myriads of broken reeds all still and stiff,
Like me who have no love which this wild rain
Has not dissolved except the love of death,
If love it be for what is perfect and
Cannot, the tempest tells me, disappoint.

LIGHTS OUT

I have come to the borders of sleep,
The unfathomable deep
Forest where all must lose
Their way, however straight,
Or winding, soon or late;
They cannot choose.

Many a road and track
That, since the dawn's first crack,
Up to the forest brink,
Deceived the travellers,
Suddenly now blurs,
And in they sink.

Here love ends,
Despair, ambition ends;
All pleasure and all trouble,
Although most sweet or bitter,
Here ends in sleep that is sweeter
Than tasks most noble.

There is not any book
Or face of dearest look
That I would not turn from now
To go into the unknown
I must enter, and leave, alone,
I know not how.

The tall forest towers;
Its cloudy foliage lowers

Ahead, shelf above shelf;
Its silence I hear and obey
That I may lose my way
And myself.

TED HUGHES

TED HUGHES

TED HUGHES was born in a mining area in the West Riding of Yorkshire in 1930. He was educated at Mexborough Grammar School and won an exhibition to Pembroke College, Cambridge where – after two years of National Service in the R.A.F. – he studied English before switching to Anthropology for his final year. In 1956 he married the American poet, the late Sylvia Plath. By that time Ted Hughes had the bulk of his first book, *The Hawk in the Rain*, ready for publication.

When it appeared his reputation was established almost at once. That fine poet and sensitive critic, Edwin Muir, spoke for many when he asserted that a remarkable new poet had appeared on the scene. 'A most surprising first book,' Edwin Muir wrote in the *New Statesman* (28th September, 1957). 'Ted Hughes seems to be quite outside the currents of his time.' By that, Muir meant Ted Hughes's poetry was quite differently ordered from that of the Movement poets so fashionable in 1957 whose work was noted for its decorum and verbal restraint. In comparison, the poems of Ted Hughes seemed primitive and dramatic and unashamed of their rhetorical energy. His diction, too, allowed his themes to be other than merely domestic, celebrating as he did so often – like D. H. Lawrence – the instinctual life.

Of course, taking a longer perspective than a year or two, the poetry of Ted Hughes was not 'outside the currents of his time'. There was, as has been indicated, a kinship with

Lawrence whose home once had also been in a mining area. Indeed Ted Hughes has said that when he first read D. H. Lawrence during his 'teens he found that it was like reading his own autobiography. Again, technically, Hughes's poetry had immediate literary antecedents – Dylan Thomas, and behind Dylan Thomas, Manley Hopkins whose roots lie in that alliterative and rhythmically intense Anglo-Saxon verse from which Ted Hughes continues to draw sustenance directly.

In 1960, *Lupercal*, Ted Hughes's second book was published. It contained so many satisfying, whole, rationally-structured poems – poems *economically* containing their energy pent up within them – that those who had been somewhat reserved about the virtues of *The Hawk in the Rain* now capitulated. Critical praise had become universal, and poems such as Hawk Roosting, View of a Pig, Thrushes, Pike, An Otter, and other 'animal' poems showed Hughes at his most controlled and at his best. 'His empathy with the animals he contemplates,' M. L. Rosenthal has written in *The New Poets*, 'is so thorough and so concretely specific that the effect is of magical incantation, a conjuring up of another possible kind of self. Both otter and pike, though they *can* be caught and killed by man, are given supernatural attributions by the language that Hughes sometimes employs in describing them, and by his awestruck feeling of the mystery of their existential reality, so different from our own though constantly suggestive of the human.'

In his 'animal' poems since *Lupercal*, Ted Hughes has given his creatures even greater preternatural attributes. The Thrushes, the Pike, and the Otter, that Hughes described in *Lupercal*, the reader will feel derived from nature and from the rapacious, atavistic mystery of nature. Some of the animal poems in his third volume *Wodwo* (1967) depict creatures as they appear in dreams or myth and are even more *threatening* figures. Consider The Bear:

34

The bear is digging
In his sleep
Through the wall of the Universe
With a man's femur.

Or The Giant Crabs which have become, in fact, Ghost Crabs:

Gradually the labouring of the tide
Falls back from its productions,
Its power slips back from glistening nacelles, and
    they are crabs.
Giant crabs, under flat skulls, staring inland
Like a packed trench of helmets.
Ghosts, they are ghost-crabs.
They emerge
An invisible disgorging of the sea's cold
Over the man who strolls along the sands.

Again, there is a powerful short story in *Wodwo* called
Rain Horse. As we might now expect, here the horse ceases to
be merely a domestic animal, 'the friend of man', but becomes
instead a malevolent, mythic beast. It is as if The Horse, The
Bear, The Giant Crabs are haunted, indeed inhabited, by
spirits from another world. More and more Ted Hughes has
moved away from poems about creatures that behave according to natural law and as they exist in nature, so that in his
most recent volume *Crow* (1970) those poems which feature
a crow as the main protagonist have quite often no earthly
connection with that bird as we know it at all. The crow has
become a non-bird, has become a figure in a terrifying, black,
private vision.

Crow is a black book full of threat, sadness, cruelty, pain,
castration, and death. Many of the poems have correspond-
ence with old runic chants, folk tales, and primitive oral
verse. A number of the poems, too, have abandoned the

rationally-structured modes apparent in his first two books. In the larger part of *Wodwo*, in such a poem as *Cadenza*, with its surrealistic excitements and images, 'The clouds are full of surgery and collisions / But the coffin escapes –' the reader may feel that reciprocal influence between Hughes's poetry and that of his late wife, Sylvia Plath, which the American poet Daniel Hoffman referred to in the Summer 1968 issue of *Shenandoah*. 'It might be proposed that if her searching breakthroughs into surreality in *Ariel* were made possible by her response to the absolute honesty and freedom from cant in his *Lupercal*, the new forays in *Wodwo* into sudden flashes of revealed truth may owe something to Sylvia Plath's example. In her poems we hear the sounds the mind makes as it snaps, the electric crackling of emotional energy leaping from the last ground logic can stand on to the place of truth it didn't know it could arrive at.'

These new forays have led from *Wodwo* to *Crow*. The few new poems he has written since then including Existential Song, The Contender, and Crow Hears Fate Knock on the Door, to be found in this selection, continue on the same route – out on a black tangent, as it were, over a black chasm. The voice of Ted Hughes is still ferocious, unhappy, and remarkable.

Nowadays the art of poetry may no longer be disruptive as it once was. We no longer respond to a poem in purely magical terms. Plato was speaking as a primitive when he held that the poet was a dangerous, disruptive force; that the poet should be honoured, anointed with myrrh, but sent on his way to another city.

We are relatively sophisticated, sophisticated enough anyway to be partly armoured against the magical ingredients of art and therefore we are unafraid of being utterly possessed by a poem as Plato was. A poem hardly makes us even momentarily mad. Nevertheless, enough vestigial 'sacred fear' of the poet persists. The strange, sacrificial metamorphosis of

Dylan Thomas – and to some extent of Sylvia Plath also – from an individual to a legend, exemplifies how people still are enthralled by certain 'sacred' things – like dead poets and dead kings.

Fortunately, Ted Hughes is very much alive. His most recent poetry particularly leans heavily 'on the magical ingredients of art'. As such, it may leave in our minds faint echoing detonations that we did not know we had heard before, and which go very far back indeed into our own unacknowledged natures.

Ted Hughes writes:

There are all sorts of ways of capturing animals and birds and fish. I spent most of my time, up to the age of 15 or so, trying out many of these ways and when my enthusiasm began to wane, as it did gradually, I started to write poems. You mightn't think that these two interests, capturing animals and writing poems, have much in common. But the more I think back, the more sure I am that with me the two interests have been one interest. My pursuit of mice at threshing time when I was a boy, snatching them from under the sheaves as the sheaves were lifted away out of the stack and popping them into my pockets till I had 30 or 40 crawling around in the lining of my coat – that and my present pursuit of poems seem to me to be different stages of the same fever. In a way, I suppose, I think of poems as a sort of animal. They have their own life, like animals, by which I mean that they seem quite separate from any person, even from their author, and nothing can be added to them or taken away without maiming and perhaps even killing them. And they have a certain wisdom. They know something special – something perhaps which we are very curious to learn. Maybe my concern has been to capture not animals particularly and not poems, but simply things which have a vivïd life of their own, outside mine. However all that may be, my interest in animals began when I began. My memory goes back pretty clearly to my third year, and by then I had so many of the toy lead animals you could buy in shops that they went right around our flat-topped fender nose to tail, with some over. . . . My zoo wasn't entirely an indoors affair. At that time we lived in a valley in the Pennines in west Yorkshire. My brother, who probably had more to do with this passion of mine than anyone else, was a good bit older than I was, and his one interest in life was creeping about on the hillsides with a rifle. He took me along as a retriever and I had to scramble into all kinds of places collecting magpies and owls and rabbits and weasels and rats and curlews that he shot. He couldn't shoot enough for me. At the same time I used to be fishing daily in the canal, with a long-handled wire-rimmed curtain-mesh sort of net.

All that was a beginning. When I was about eight, we moved to an industrial town in south Yorkshire. Our cat went upstairs and moped in my bedroom for a week, it hated the place so much, and my brother for the same reason left home and became a gamekeeper. But in many ways that move of ours was the best thing that ever happened to me. I soon discovered a farm in the nearby country that supplied all my needs, and a private estate, with woods and lake. I still have some diaries that I kept in those years: they record nothing but my catches. Every weekend there was something, often during the week too: and during holidays there was something every day. At the same time I bred coloured mice, rabbits, guinea pigs and so on, as most boys do. Finally, as I have said, at about 15 my life grew more complicated and my attitude to animals changed. I accused myself of disturbing their lives. I began to look at them from their own point of view.

And about the same time I began to write poems. Not animal poems. It was years before I wrote what you could call an animal poem, and several more years before it occurred to me that my writing poems might be largely a continuation of my earlier pursuit. Now I have no doubt. The special kind of excitement, the slightly mesmerized and quite involuntary concentration, with which you make out the stirrings of a new poem in your mind, then the outline, the mass and colour and clean final form of it, the unique living reality of it in the midst of the general lifelessness – all that is too familiar to mistake. This is hunting and the poem is a new species of creature, a new specimen of the life outside your own.

(From *Poetry in the Making* (Faber))

*   *   *

The poet's only hope is to be infinitely sensitive to what his gift is, and this in itself seems to be another gift that few poets possess. According to this sensitivity, and to his faith in it, he will go on developing as a poet, as Yeats did, pursuing those adventures, mental, spiritual and physical, whatever they may be, that his gift wants, or he will lose its guidance, lose the feel of its touch in the workings of his mind, and soon be absorbed by the impersonal dead lumber of matters in which his gift has no interest, which is a form of suicide, metaphorical in the case of Wordsworth and Coleridge, actual in the case of Mayakovsky. . . .

The poet's gift is an unobliging thing. He can study his art, experiment, and apply his mind and live as he pleases. But the moment of writing is too late for further improvements or adjustments. Certain memories, images, sounds, feelings, thoughts, and relationships between these, have for some reason become luminous at the core of his mind: it is in his attempt to bring them out, without impairment, into a comparatively dark world that he makes poems. At the moment of writing, the poetry is a combination, or a resultant, of all that he is, unimpeachable evidence of itself and, indirectly, of himself, and for the time of writing he can do nothing but accept it. If he doesn't approve of what is appearing, there are always plenty of ways to falsify and 'improve' it, there are always plenty of fashions as to how it should look, how it can be made more acceptable, more 'interesting', his other faculties are only too ready to load it with their business, whereon he ceases to be a poet producing what poetry he can and becomes a cheat producing confusion.

(From The London Magazine)

WIND

This house has been far out at sea all night,
The woods crashing through darkness, the booming hills,
Winds stampeding the fields under the window
Floundering black astride and blinding wet

Till day rose; then under an orange sky
The hills had new places, and wind wielded
Blade-light, luminous black and emerald,
Flexing like the lens of a mad eye.

At noon I scaled along the house-side as far as
The coal-house door. I dared once to look up –
Through the brunt wind that dented the balls of my eyes
The tent of the hills drummed and strained its guyrope,

The fields quivering, the skyline a grimace,
At any second to bang and vanish with a flap:
The wind flung a magpie away and a black-
Back gull bent like an iron bar slowly. The house

Rang like some fine green goblet in the note
That any second would shatter it. Now deep
In chairs, in front of the great fire, we grip
Our hearts and cannot entertain book, thought,

Or each other. We watch the fire blazing,
And feel the roots of the house move, but sit on,
Seeing the window tremble to come in,
Hearing the stones cry out under the horizons.

WITCHES

Once was every woman the witch
To ride a weed the ragwort road;
Devils to do whatever she would:
Each rosebud, every old bitch.

Did they bargain their bodies or no?
Proprietary the devil that
Went horsing on their every thought
When they scowled the strong and lucky low.

Dancing in Ireland nightly, gone
To Norway (the ploughboy bridled),
Nightlong under the blackamoor spraddled,
Back beside their spouse by dawn

As if they had dreamed all. Did they dream it?
Oh, our science says they did.
It was all wishfully dreamed in bed.
Small psychology would unseam it.

Bitches still sulk, rosebuds blow,
And we are devilled. And though these weep
Over our harms, who's to know
Where their feet dance while their heads sleep?

HAWK ROOSTING

I sit in the top of the wood, my eyes closed.
Inaction, no falsifying dream
Between my hooked head and hooked feet:
Or in sleep rehearse perfect kills and eat.

The convenience of the high trees!
The air's buoyancy and the sun's ray
Are of advantage to me;
And the earth's face upward for my inspection.

My feet are locked upon the rough bark.
It took the whole of Creation
To produce my foot, my each feather:
Now I hold Creation in my foot

Or fly up, and revolve it all slowly –
I kill where I please because it is all mine.
There is no sophistry in my body:
My manners are tearing off heads –

The allotment of death.
For the one path of my flight is direct
Through the bones of the living.
No arguments assert my right:

The sun is behind me.
Nothing has changed since I began.
My eye has permitted no change.
I am going to keep things like this.

VIEW OF A PIG

The pig lay on a barrow dead.
It weighed, they said, as much as three men.
Its eyes closed, pink white eyelashes.
Its trotters stuck straight out.

Such weight and thick pink bulk
Set in death seemed not just dead.
It was less than lifeless, further off.
It was like a sack of wheat.

I thumped it without feeling remorse.
One feels guilty insulting the dead,
Walking on graves. But this pig
Did not seem able to accuse.

It was too dead. Just so much
A poundage of lard and pork.
Its last dignity had entirely gone.
It was not a figure of fun.

Too dead now to pity.
To remember its life, din, stronghold
Of earthly pleasure as it had been,
Seemed a false effort, and off the point.

Too deadly factual. Its weight
Oppressed me – how could it be moved?
And the trouble of cutting it up!
The gash in its throat was shocking, but not pathetic.

Once I ran at a fair in the noise
To catch a greased piglet
That was faster and nimbler than a cat,
Its squeal was the rending of metal.

Pigs must have hot blood, they feel like ovens.
Their bite is worse than a horse's –
They chop a half-moon clean out.
They eat cinders, dead cats.

Distinctions and admirations such
As this one was long finished with.
I stared at it a long time. They were going to scald it,
Scald it and scour it like a doorstep.

CADENZA

The violinist's shadow vanishes.

The husk of a grasshopper
Sucks a remote cyclone and rises.

The full, bared throat of a woman walking water,
The loaded estuary of the dead.

And I am the cargo
Of a coffin attended by swallows.

And I am the water
Bearing the coffin that will not be silent.

The clouds are full of surgery and collisions
But the coffin escapes – as a black diamond,

A ruby brimming blood,
An emerald beating its shores,

The sea lifts swallow wings and flings
A summer lake open,

Sips and bewilders its reflection,
Till the whole sky dives shut like a burned land back
    to its spark –

A bat with a ghost in its mouth
Struck at by lightnings of silence –

Blue with sweat, the violinist
Crashes into the orchestra, which explodes.

CROW TYRANNOSAURUS

Creation quaked voices –
It was a cortege
Of mourning and lament
Crow could hear and he looked around fearfully.

The swift's body fled past
Pulsating
With insects
And their anguish, all it had eaten.

The cat's body writhed
Gagging
A tunnel
Of incoming death-struggles, sorrow on sorrow.

And the dog was a bulging filterbag
Of all the deaths it had gulped for the flesh and the bones.
It could not digest their screeching finales.
Its shapeless cry was a blort of all those voices.

Even man he was a walking
Abattoir
Of innocents –
His brain incinerating their outcry.

Crow thought 'Alas
Alas ought I
To stop eating
And try to become the light?'

But his eye saw a grub. And his head, trapsprung, stabbed.
And he listened
And he heard
Weeping

Grubs   grubs   He stabbed   he stabbed
Weeping
Weeping

Weeping he walked and stabbed

Thus came the eye's

                roundness

                      the ear's

                          deafness.

CROW HEARS FATE KNOCK ON THE DOOR

Crow looked at the world, mountainously heaped.
He looked at the heavens, littering away
Beyond every limit.
He looked in front of his feet at the little stream
Chugging on like an auxiliary motor
Fastened to this infinite engine.

He imagined the whole engineering
Of its assembly, repairs and maintenance –
And felt helpless.

He plucked grass-heads and gazed into them
Waiting for first instructions.
He studied a stone from the stream.
He found a dead mole and slowly he took it apart,
Then stared at the gobbets, feeling helpless.
He walked, he walked
Letting the translucent starry spaces
Blow in his ear cluelessly.

Yet the prophecy inside him, like a grimace,
Was I will measure it all, and own it all,
And I will be inside it
As inside my own laughter
And not staring out at it through walls
Of my eye's cold quarantine
From a buried cell of bloody blackness –

This prophecy was inside him, like a steel spring

Slowly rending the vital fibres.

THE CONTENDER

There was this man and he was the strongest
Of the strong.
He gritted his teeth like a cliff.
Though his body was sweeling away like a torrent on a
    cliff
Smoking towards dark gorges
There he nailed himself with nails of nothing

All the women in the world could not move him
They came their mouths deformed against stone
They came and their tears salted his nail-holes
Only adding their embitterment
To his effort
He abandoned his grin to them his grimace
In his face upwards body he lay face downwards
As a dead man adamant

His sandals could not move him they burst their thongs
And rotted from his fixture
All the men in the world could not move him
They wore at him with their shadows and little sounds
Their arguments were a relief
Like heather flowers
His belt could not endure the siege – it burst
And lay broken
He grinned
Little children came in chorus to move him
But he glanced at them out of his eye-corners
Over the edge of his grin
And they lost their courage for life

Oak forests came and went with the hawk's wing
Mountains rose and fell
He lay crucified with all his strength
On the earth
Grinning towards the sun
Through the tiny holes of his eyes
And towards the moon
And towards the whole paraphernalia of the heavens
Through the seams of his face
With the strings of his lips
Grinning through his atoms and decay
Grinning into the black
Into the ringing nothing
Through the bones of his teeth

Sometimes with eyes closed

In his senseless trial of strength.

EXISTENTIAL SONG

Once upon a time
There was a person
Running for his life.
This was his fate.
It was a hard fate.
But Fate is Fate.
He had to keep running.

He began to wonder about Fate
And running for dear life.
Who? Why?
And was he nothing
But some dummy hare on a racetrack?

At last he made up his mind.
He was nobody's fool.
It would take guts
But yes he could do it.
Yes yes he could stop.
Agony! Agony
Was the wrenching
Of himself from his running.
Vast! And sudden
The stillness
In the empty middle of the desert.

There he stood – stopped.
And since he couldn't see anybody
To North or to West or to East or to South
He raised his fists
Laughing in awful joy
And shook them at the Universe

And his fists fell off
And his arms fell off
He staggered and his legs fell off

It was too late for him to realize
That this was the dogs tearing him to pieces
That he was, in fact, nothing
But a dummy hare on a racetrack.

And life was being lived only by the dogs.

SONG AGAINST THE WHITE OWL

The white owl got its proof weapons
Bequests of its victims.

And it got those eyes that look beyond life
From fluorescence of old corpses.

It snatched its bones as it could
From the burning of blizzard.

Death loans it a belly.
It wears a face it found on the sea.

Twisting sinew of last breaths
It bent these oddments together.

With a ghostly needle of screech
It sewed a coat of the snow

From the knobbed and staring ice
Wringing blood and fat.

O stare Owl stare
Through your glacier wall
At a fatal terrain
Of weeping snow and the leaf of the birch

Where I spoon your soul from a bowl
And my song steams.

DAVID WRIGHT

DAVID WRIGHT

DESPITE David Wright being one of the half dozen best poets of a gifted generation, his work in latter years has been somewhat neglected. He has not been represented in various popular anthologies; he has been excluded from occasional surveys of contemporary poetry; he is not invited to appear at any of the many poetry readings that now take place up and down the country. The latter exclusion is the only one that is understandable for David Wright is completely deaf – though it may be mentioned here that his attractive actress wife, Philippa Reid, when persuaded to appear on such platforms, will recite his poems with particular sensitivity.

David Wright was born in Johannesburg in 1920, an only child of comfortably off parents. His childhood, until the age of seven, appears to have been idyllic. But in 1927 he contracted scarlet fever which at that time, since there were no antibiotics, was a dangerous disease. It left David Wright permanently and completely deaf. In the autobiographical section of his book, *Deafness*, David Wright characteristically comments, 'My becoming deaf when I did – if deafness had to be my destiny – was remarkably lucky. By the age of seven a child will have grasped the essentials of language, as I had. Having learnt naturally how to speak was another advantage – pronunciation, syntax, inflection, idiom, all had come by ear. I had the basis of a vocabulary which could easily be extended by reading. All these would have been denied me had I been born deaf or lost my hearing earlier than I did. Lastly I was too young to be disorientated or emotionally incommoded by the loss, whilst still young enough to adapt to the disability without effort . . .'

This affirmative note is one that is refreshingly present in many of his poems and seems to spring from a celebratory religious sensibility. Thus in that fine poem, 'Monologue of a Deaf Man', David Wright asserts:

In whatever condition, whole, blind, dumb,
One-legged or leprous, the human being is,
I affirm the human condition is the same,
The heart half broken in ashes and in lies
But sustained by the immensity of the divine.

Thus I too must praise out of a quiet ear
The great creation to which I owe I am
My grief and my love. O hear me if I cry
Among the din of birds deaf to their acclaim,
Involved like them in the not unhearing air.

It was because of his deafness that David Wright, at the age of thirteen, left South Africa. He wished to gain a university education eventually and could best do this by studying in Northampton, England, in a special, private, middle class school for the deaf and dumb which had gained, before it closed down in 1944, 'an academic record second to none in the deaf world'. In 1939 he achieved his ambition to go to Oxford having passed an examination for one of the three vacant places at Oriel.

Before studying at Oxford, David Wright had read very little 'modern' poetry indeed. Like other poet undergraduates of those early war years, though, he came under the influence of Sidney Keyes who introduced him to the hortatory work of romantic poets like Dylan Thomas and Vernon Watkins. As David Wright has confessed, 'Keyes's poetry – at the time he was scarcely nineteen – was extraordinarily assured and polished: it hypnotized his contemporaries. Sooner or later everyone, including me, found himself writing Keyesian poems . . .'

David Wright did not shed his early poetic influences until long after he left Oxford, not in fact till a decade later. His second book of poems, *Moral Stories* (1954), however, was almost entirely in his own manner: dryly humorous, anecdotal, elegant, yet still laced with colloquialisms, and most mysteriously, not only aurally correct, but aurally adventurous. These qualities continue to be apparent in his later works, *Monologue of a Deaf Man* (1958), *Adam at Evening* (1965), and *Nerve Ends* (1969).

On hearing David Wright speak the listener cannot help but notice that from time to time Mr. Wright will pronounce occasional words peculiarly, putting the accent on the wrong syllable. After all, there are many words in his surprisingly large vocabulary that he has never heard pronounced. How then, one may well ask, can he write rhythmic verses with such assurance and subtlety? David Wright, himself, in *Deafness*, draws attention to that inexplicable quality in poetry which allows it to survive in different pronunciations. 'It is known that the pronunciation of English has changed over the centuries,' David Wright reminds us. 'If we had a record of Pope reading 'The Rape of the Lock' he would sound queer, and Shakespeare speaking one of his sonnets queerer yet, while Chaucer might be unintelligible. But the sound-effects of their verse do not seem impaired by modern pronunciation.'

I have never heard David Wright read his own poems – such an occasion might make me mistake him for Chaucer for all I know. What I am certain of is that his poems when read out loud by others give no hint that the author is a deaf man any more than the late music of Beethoven suggests that that composer was similarly afflicted.

Probably the most affecting poems David Wright has

written have sprung from his personal predicament of deafness: triumphantly in 'Monologue of a Deaf Man'; touchingly in 'By the Effigy of St. Cecilia' (the patron saint of music); and tersely in a poem called, 'On Himself':

> Abstracted by silence from the age of seven,
> Deafened and penned by as black calamity
> As twice to be born, I cannot without pity
> Contemplate myself as an infant;
>
> Or fail to speak of silence as a priestess
> Calling to serve in the temple of a skull
> Her innocent choice. It is barely possible
> Not to be affected by such a distress.

Perhaps it is his deafness, his own sense of otherness that allows him, with greater facility than some, to identify with those living on the margins of society, with the one-legged and the leprous, with the self-exiled Soho Bohemian, with the different and the hurt. His recent removal from London to the country in Cumberland has led him to a new source of imagery, but the same quality of reasoning compassion that informed his earlier work now operates in this new context and allows him to write poems like 'Swift', and 'Rook'.

David Wright has always been the man outside, the sly observer with a decorative verbal gift, one who is moreover willing to laugh at himself and at us, but it is in such *feeling* poems as these, written it would appear out of an actual autobiographical pressure, that he is at his best. He may say that he is committed to his notion of the Absurd (any man born in South Africa is entitled to say that), but beyond such a stance, when he himself is directly and feelingly involved with that which he is witnessing, his poetry becomes more than mere electric description and decorative comment for it reaches out instead to its broadest and true dimensions.

———————

David Wright writes:

The best a poet can say for, about, or against his own work
will be found in his poems. Or perhaps his critical assessments
of other people's poetry – in the sense that Eliot's essay on
Dante throws almost more light on the poetry of T. S. Eliot
than it does on *La Divina Commedia*.

So it seems to me that the most relevant contribution to
offer as regards my own verse is to remark that the man who
wrote it was born in South Africa in 1920, became deaf at
the age of seven, escaped a standardized education, spent the
war years at Oxford and in Soho, married an actress from
New Zealand, and at one time or another had the benefit of
meeting and learning from David Gascoyne, John Heath-
Stubbs, Roy Campbell, George Barker, Patrick Kavanagh
and Hugh MacDiarmid. These accidents and people helped
to shape the mould in which the poems were cast.

Like most people I began to write verse because I enjoyed
reading poetry. So far as I remember my first rhymes were
mated in an attic flat off Paddington when I was on a visit to
England to do a round of the ear specialists. I had been deaf
for a year and one reason why I liked poetry may have been
the fact that I found in it a substitute for the music I could no
longer listen to. The auditory element in poetry has always
appealed to me more than the visual.

Language also has been my obsession, though all poets
love language (probably the only safe generalization one can
make about poets). But it is spoken rather than written
language that fascinates, as being the harder to come by – at
least where I am concerned – and so more prized. Not that I
object to a literary rhetoric, e.g. Milton's latinized eloquence.
Though I prefer the poetry of John Clare to the poetry of
John Keats, and if pushed would say that it is because Clare's
is nearer common speech. But I have no theories about poetry.

Which is a lie of course. Poetry is all or nothing: 'If it is not more than very well, it is very bad, there is no intermediate state,' as Wordsworth, who should know, remarked. A poem either works or it doesn't. Even then that may be for a short time only – a day, a year, a decade, a generation. Look how curled at the edges a lot of self-consciously 'modern poetry' of the twenties and thirties now seems, compared with the apparently traditionalistic stuff of Edward Thomas. Not that the traditionalistic is the answer. There is no stylistic recipe for the concoction of a poem.

That is, if the aim be to produce a poem that works for now and will go on working for autres temps, autres moeurs. All art is about this problem. This is why no art is a modest art, least of all the art of poetry, *pace* some contemporaries who say that it is.

It can't be achieved simply by hard work and the earnest application of verbal, prosodic, or structural techniques and sleights, though these help where they don't hinder. Here enters mystery. This is what the craftsman Yeats meant when he said that a poem is a piece of luck. To make a poem is not to make an artefact but a living entity, to make life. Like God, the poet can only pass it on, breathe in a bit of his own.

This is a different thing from self-expression though near enough for confusion. Anybody can express himself more or less badly. But to invest one's personality, or individual apprehension of the visible and invisible world in images made of paint or stone or language – 'blood, imagination, intellect running together' – so that they walk away existing in their own right, like children, individual in themselves even if recognizably endowed with the parental qualities and imperfections, that is quite another fish-kettle.

For this it is not enough to have 'personality'. What is needed, I suppose, is the 'negative capability' Keats talked about.

The necessary trick is ability to set down aspects of reality.

Any reality, there are no grades of importance. 'Snatch out of time the passionate transitory' Kavanagh asked in his poem about the functional ward of a chest hospital. This has nothing to do with a talent for representation or description. I think of those marvellous figures by Giovanni Pisano, pocked and blurred by hundreds of years of good and bad weather, where the movement of the human body continues, exists, has not been merely represented. An aspect of reality translated into stone. In poetry the same ability or gift is required. It demands, I believe, a hard kind of detachment. The personal vision is easily distorted by the cataract of the ego. It's not a question of sincerity, any fool can be sincere (most fools are). As an aspect of the real, insincerity is also valid.

MONOLOGUE OF A DEAF MAN

Et lui comprit trop bien, n'ayant pas entendu.
Tristan Corbière

It is a good plan, and began with childhood
As my fortune discovered, only to hear
How much it is necessary to have said.
Oh silence, independent of a stopped ear,
You observe birds, flying, sing with wings instead.

Then do you console yourself? You are consoled
If you are, as all are. So easy a youth
Still unconcerned with the concern of a world
Where, masked and legible, a moment of truth
Manifests what, gagged, a tongue should have told;

Still observer of vanity and courage
And of these mirror as well; that is something
More than a sound of violin to assuage
What the human being most dies of: boredom
Which makes hedgebirds clamour in their blackthorn
  cage.

But did the brushless fox die of eloquence?
No, but talked himself, it seems, into a tale.
The injury, dominated, is an asset;
It is there for domination, that is all.
Else what must faith do deserted by mountains?

Talk to me then, you who have so much to say,
Spectator of the human conversation,

Reader of tongues, examiner of the eye,
And detective of clues in every action,
What could a voice, if you heard it, signify?

The tone speaks less than a twitch and a grimace.
People make to depart, do not say 'Goodbye'.
Decision, indecision, drawn on every face
As if they spoke. But what do they really say?
You are not spared, either, the banalities.

In whatever condition, whole, blind, dumb,
One-legged or leprous, the human being is,
I affirm the human condition is the same,
The heart half broken in ashes and in lies,
But sustained by the immensity of the divine.

Thus I too must praise out of a quiet ear
The great creation to which I owe I am
My grief and my love. O hear me if I cry
Among the din of birds deaf to their acclaim,
Involved like them in the not unhearing air.

BY THE EFFIGY OF ST. CECILIA

Having peculiar reverence for this creature
Of the numinous imagination, I am come
To visit her church and stand before the altar
Where her image, hewn in pathetic stone,
Exhibits the handiwork of her executioner.

There are the axemarks. Outside, in the courtyard,
In shabby habit, an Italian nun
Came up and spoke: I had to answer, 'Sordo.'
She said she was a teacher of deaf children
And had experience of my disorder.

And I have had experience of her order,
Interpenetrating chords and marshalled sound;
Often I loved to listen to the organ's
Harmonious and concordant interpretation
Of what is due from us to the creation.

But it was taken from me in my childhood
And those graduated pipes turned into stone.
Now, having travelled a long way through silence,
Within the church in Trastevere I stand
A pilgrim to the patron saint of music

And am abashed by the presence of this nun
Beside the embodiment of that legendary
Virgin whose music and whose martyrdom
Is special to this place: by her reality.
She is a reminder of practical kindness,

The care it takes to draw speech from the dumb
Or pierce with sense the carapace of deafness;
And so, of the plain humility of the ethos
That constructed, also, this elaborate room
To pray for bread in; they are not contradictory.

A FUNERAL ORATION

Composed at thirty, my funeral oration: Here lies
David John Murray Wright, 6' 2", myopic blue eyes;
Hair grey (very distinguished looking, so I am told);
Shabbily dressed as a rule; susceptible to cold;
Acquainted with what are known as the normal vices;
Perpetually short of cash; useless in a crisis;
Preferring cats, hated dogs; drank (when he could) too
    much;
Was deaf as a tombstone; and extremely hard to touch.
Academic achievements: B.A., Oxon (2nd class);
Poetic: the publication of one volume of verse,
Which in his thirtieth year attained him no fame at all
Except among intractable poets, and a small
Lunatic fringe congregating in Soho pubs.
He could roll himself cigarettes from discarded stubs,
Assume the first position of Yoga; sail, row, swim;
And though deaf, in church appear to be joining a hymn.
Often arrested for being without a permit,
Starved on his talents as much as he dined on his wit,
Born in a dominion to which he hoped not to go back
Since predisposed to imagine white possibly black:
His life, like his times, was appalling; his conduct odd;
He hoped to write one good line; died believing in God.

MORAL STORY II

I met Poetry, an old prostitute walking
Along Piccadilly, one whom no one would buy,
Just a draggletail bitch with padding for each breast, –
No wonder the corner boys were gay and joking!
She'd laid on paint too thick in a colour too high,
And scuttled like a red hen deprived of its nest.

But she stopped for a word with me, one of her pimps,
Her faithful old ponce still hoping for his percent.
When I asked, 'How's business?' she shook her leary
    head:
'In peacetime the boys are not so keen on the nymphs;
'And I am getting a bit behind with the rent.
'These days the pickings are small that fall from my bed.

'Wartime was whoretime! Never mind, cheer up, lovey;
'Find me another fee like the one from New York:
'They pay very nicely, the Yanks – and don't look glum.
' – Or go get another girl, if you want more gravy!'
She screamed, ' – you've got your good looks yet, – or
    you could work!
'Go get yourself a job licking somebody's bum!'

But out of the corner of my eye I'd seen a Rolls Royce
Purr by us with a back seat full of her old friends,
Passing, like the gent in the song, the girl they'd ruined.
They lifted a disdainful nostril at her noise,
And continued, as you might expect, to pursue their
    ends,
With cigars drawing, and the radio carefully tuned

To a highbrow programme. So across the gutter
We caught one another's look; and as their exhaust
Echoed outside of the Ritz like a burst paper bag,
Laughed like hyenas; she, with a shaking udder,
Said, 'I was a lovely piece, when they met me first!'
And lineaments of desire lit the old hag.

THE DEVISER

With what extraordinary delights he
Informs his creation – what madness is in
His ideas for vegetable propagation!
That remarkable arrangement between a bee

And a rose would not occur to an engineer.
To me a rose looks beautiful, but I imagine
It is desirable merely to the busy one
Up to his honeybags in a petal vagina.

A rose is no good to me except to look at.
Between the human legs there is a crop of hair
Which I find delectable but cannot admire
Merely, as in the case of a rose, in the abstract.

Like the insect, I too have my honeypot,
One that it would not occur to me to devise
With such thrift, considering the various
Other uses to which it is put,

Some of which I have no taste for. But I suppose
He is not going to let us forget we came from
The dirt he shaped his image of, if Adam
Was his image and not the world that is.

All the same one has to admit the set-up is odd.
After making every allowance for his delight
I do not understand why joy should permeate
All his devices and each expedient.

AS YOU WERE SAYING
To Dannie Abse

I agree, Dannie, it's not important to know
The cognomens and purposes of greenery
Or birds (it's always a chaffinch or a sparrow;
Seagulls, I suppose, like blackbirds, are too easy).
The painter Rothenstein took Yeats for a walk
And found the visible world did not inspire
The poet, who apparently failed to remark
The abundant natural beauty of Gloucestershire,
But fixed his eyes on his boots and talked about
His concerns, which were not the noise of birds and water,
Or the sun, or the wilder wildflowers, or the wind on
   the heath . . .
The etceteras of nature preen and bloom.
                        – But the myopic
Celebrant of phenomena does not see them.

I live in the country now, having left London,
And find myself, very much to my surprise,
Reconnoitring the surrounding vegetation,
The local wildlife and even the night skies;
But not for the sake of poetry, thank goodness.
These things have forced themselves on me, being there.
One may as well find out about them. Who knows,
A night will come when I'll have need of the pole star.

RHAPSODY OF A MIDDLE-AGED MAN

These are the middle years, and I attend
Experience and the dying of the heart.
I don't feel melancholy. The idea of an end
To the world that I am cheers me up.
Only I used to feel, before, what now I know.
Enjoying more, I care for less and less,
And cherish what I do not understand –
The gaiety at the heart of mysteries.

What astonishes most is to look back and find
That there is really nothing to regret.
O my lost despairs! Where, where have you died?
Why did you go away and send me no report?
I see there is achievement in a leaf
Because it broke the bud, courage in a wall
Because it stands; a beatitude in grief
– Committed as I am to the absurd.

How can I take the universe as solemn
Seeing it's prodigal, wastes and spends,
Has no concern with thrift or responsibility
Any more than a hero with a roll of fivers
On a Saturday night taking care of his friends.
The unselective benevolence is disquieting.
What about tomorrow and the final reckoning?
He won't worry, he's the final reckoning.

As one grows older one gets caught up more
In the precipitate irresponsible gaiety.
I ought to spare time to consider the bomb

And the likelihood of no future for humanity.
But spring comes along, and trees burst into banknotes,
Or I am observing the delicate limbs of a fly
Sampling a lump of sugar on a café table.
The singing nightingales had no time for Agamemnon.

There are no consolations, none are required.
The fury and despair are the vanity.
I see the exhilaration of the numinous
Regard the tears that we shed with a dry eye.
Alas, what happened? Am I no longer sensitive?
What took my tragic gown and crown away?
What leaves me standing like a fool in the huge
Gale of the universe, naked to joy?

The godhead is in the instant of being,
The Niagara of our squandered time
Sculpting its form in the movement of its falling.
No one drop more precious than the others gone
Looking for the matches, making love or a poem,
Waiting for the bus or an old age pension.
I am not called to balance such accounts or fear
Whether the waste is worth the prospect I admire.

Still one ought to end on the serious note.
I can see a number of attitudes to strike.
The trouble is they seem fundamentally comic.
And, when one thinks, it is easier to invest
In lacrimae rerum. You get a good dividend.
But how can I pull the heartstrings of a harp
I can no longer use in the ironic midday.
When he came out of hell what tune did Orpheus play,
Was it delight or frenzy that tore his bones apart?

BOM JESUS

On the stairway leading up to the Bom Jesus,
Shrugging along on her knees, a woman in black
Paying a penance imposed on the superstitious,
Pauses to stare. I am too polite to stare back.

I descend the hillside with one hand on a camera
And the other laid upon a balustrading.
Its eighteenth-century architect was a master,
Although his church at the top seems to lack feeling.

Effigies stare from pedestals at the valley,
Lichen has given their stone the colour of calm.
Box and rhododendron have been planted carefully
And I admire the interpolation of their green

Signatures beside the stairway. Formally mounting,
Delicately harnessing geometry to praise
The idea of order as vouchsafed to the human,
Embroidering in stone a logic of line and curve,

Parting and meeting, a minuet, its flights ascend
Through a population of apostles and sages,
At every level a fountain, on every hand
A scatter of paradises.

Below stretch the vineyards: there is a city and
A river flicking the sun's light back at my eye.
Garden of felicity, for it is a garden,
With boredom the only burden if burden it be.

But painfully crawling and praying the woman
Shuffles up to Bom Jesus. The credulous
Believe in a resurrection and in heaven.
For them the stairway has been built with a purpose.

As for me I am able to photograph it,
Enjoy its baroque fountains and seduction
Of my aesthetic susceptibilities.
I have not got belief, and live in freedom.

SWIFT

A peculiar dropout, a small fledgling swift,
Stayed with us for a while as a kind of guest.
Voracious, he sat on his belly all day
Squeaking as high as a bat, except when fed.

Streamlined for flight, yet too topheavy to fly
Or take to the air in which he was meant to live,
How might he leave the ground, though designed
 for the sky?
Happy to squeak and eat, he made no attempt.

Feet like talons, powerful to cling and grip,
The hooded greedy face of a predator,
He gobbled his meat like a dragon, remained fat,
Satisfied and demanding, until one day

The scimitar wings for no reason suddenly
Beat ten times to the second. He upended
Himself with furious flutters; keeled half over
Battering with black feathers at the level

Tabletop he'd been squatting on, and almost
Stood on his head. Nothing would keep him quiet.
Having made clear to us that his time had come
He was ready to go, our pensioner of a fortnight.

We fetched him out to a field, carried in the palm
Of a hand; bowled the soft body like a ball
Into the air, which received him falling, but
His wings found their element, then scissoring

With panic sleight, bore the surprised and able
Creature to his inheritance; who sank,
Lifted and sank, with fear and confidence
Exulting into the distance, out of our sight.

ROOK

I

Tumbling across a field like a hat blown off
He made for the rookery – run, stumble, flap,
Flap, flap; but as I gained on him gave up

Suddenly, and lay calm with a confident eye,
Anaesthetized for death. Sentimentality!
I should have left him for a fox's dinner.

Began a posthumous life for this rook
Whose dead wing – broken, perhaps, by a gunshot –
Dragged buckled feathers, grounding him for good.

Yet not quite. With an admirable jealous
Obdurateness, arrogant to stay alive,
He adapted to his luck; learned to manage

That hobbled, unbalanced limb; to climb a ladder
Hop, hop, up to the porch-eaves, or unsteadier
Branches of a garden tree: comic endeavour!

Independent, indomitable, therefore clown,
Obstinate in endurance on one wing,
Stuck to a bough though wind must blow him down.

II

Salvaged by us, nursed, partly tamed, here sheltering,
A rook with four white feathers and a broken wing.

He ought to be put down, he will never again fly;
Death would be better for the bird, logically.
Nature was arranging it: starvation or a fox.
The write-off could have served a practical purpose
Fertilizing a field, or in something's stomach
Subsuming further life. The crippled rook
Cannot forage; we furnish him water and food.
Our sentimental intelligence interfered
With his despatch, created a pensioner
No use to himself or us, except to flatter
Our charity. A monster, a posthumous bird:
If the world were perfect he would now be dead.

In this aberration of the natural order
The rook bears some guilt. He is collaborator
With those who wrongly keep him alive. He could go,
Find his own death. He is not captive. But no.
Though never to take the air he means to live.
This hobble-wing, bright eye, black-purple plumage
Intently selfish, determined against pity.

SIDNEY KEYES

SIDNEY KEYES

SIDNEY KEYES was born in Dartford, Kent, in 1922. He was educated at Dartford Grammar School, Tonbridge School, and entered Queen's College, Oxford, to read history in 1940 when the Battle of Britain was still being fought in the air.

At this time, aged 18½, Sidney Keyes was already well-built, of medium height. He spoke slowly with a deep voice and gazed at everybody and everything with large, luminous hazel eyes. (Indeed a contemporary of his at Oxford, Philip Larkin, described his eyes as 'disturbing'.) With another Oxford friend, Michael Meyer, he edited *The Cherwell* and *Eight Oxford Poets* and it was during this period too that he met two strikingly beautiful girls, Milein Cosman and Renée-Jane Scott who then shared a studio and who were soon to figure in his tragically short life.

His first book of poems, *The Iron Laurel*, was published by Routledge in 1942. By this time Keyes had left Oxford, having been called up for active service in the Army. His second volume, *The Cruel Solstice*, was delivered to his publishers the following year, 1943, but before it was published Keyes, still only 20 years of age, was killed in action in Tunisia. He did not return from a reconnaissance patrol and must have run into advanced German troops.

In 1945, Michael Meyer edited and introduced Sidney Keyes's *Collected Poems* (Routledge) which immediately received critical acclaim. However, as Keyes's biographer, John Guenther, has pointed out recently, 'Keyes' work was praised for the wrong reasons after his death – people wanted a war poet, a ritual sacrifice like Rupert Brooke whose work he detested – and today he (Keyes) is largely neglected and almost forgotten.'

Sidney Keyes' poetry, as might be expected in one so young, was much concerned with Death. Besides it was war-time, Keyes had a romantic temperament, and both his personal history and his future prospects were such that it is not surprising that his poems were Death-haunted. This preoccupation with Death is evidenced not only in his poems but also in his notebook entries and in letters received by his friends.

Thus in his notebook he wrote, 'To the Middle Ages and the Elizabethans death was merely the Leveller; to the 17th Century, a metaphysical problem; to the 18th century, the end of Life. The Romantics tried to think of it as a state of existence. By the 1840s this had become an obsession and had degenerated into curiosity. By the later 19th century, and up to our own time, it had resulted in a clearly apparent Death Wish, as the only solution to the problem – since the solution must come in sensual terms.'

Again, in a letter to his friend, the poet, John Heath Stubbs, Keyes discusses the death wish in German culture and though he condemns such necrophilic desires, between the lines we can see how he remains fascinated by them. 'I think any German reader will agree,' he wrote to John Heath Stubbs in February, 1943, 'that there is a persistent death wish in German poetry; it finds its highest form in Rilke's conception. ... But the theme is constant (the whining and whimpering of Mozart's Clarinet Quintet is almost the shudder of a girl touched by her lover) and appears in painting (Matthias Grunewald) as well; it is quite unmistakable in the religious yearning of Novalis as in the rawhead, graveyard elegies of Gryphis. How can we account for the fact that a whole nation has now gone stark mad with love of death? Because the contemporary German attitude to death appears to be one of hopeless infatuation (mixed with fear and repulsion, but all physical infatuation must be) the whole nation has gone crazy with this passion, always present but now becoming overriding. . . . Perhaps the Germans are, in a sense, a chosen people; their task is to explore death, just as it has been that of the Jews to explore pain, and of the French (perhaps) to explore the possibilities of pleasure, whether of the intellect or of the senses; and to make an art of death, as the Jews have of martyrdom and the French of pleasure . . .'

Certainly his own poetry was influenced by the German poet, Rainer Maria Rilke, – not only in Rilke's attitude to Death (Rilke believed that each individual carried within him his own unique personal death that all the time was maturing like an embryo and waiting to be born) but also in Rilke's symbolic method. Sometimes the correspondences were too close. Compare, for example, these lines of Rilke:

> Put out my eyes and I can see you still
> Shut my ears and I can hear you yet
> and without any feet can go to you
> and tongueless, I can conjure you at will.
> Break off my arms I shall take hold of you
> to grasp you with my heart as with a hand.
> Arrest my heart my brain will pulse as true;
> and if you set this brain of mine on fire
> then in my blood I still will carry you.

with this short poem, A Hope for Those Separated by War, by Sidney Keyes:

> They crossed her face with blood.
> They hung her heart.
> They dragged her through a pit
> Full of quick sorrow,
> Yet her small feet
> Ran back on the morrow.

They took his book and caged
His mind in a dark house
They took his bright eyes
To light their rooms of doubt
Yet his thin hands
Crawled back and found her out.

Had Sidney Keyes survived the war, however, undoubtedly
he would have rid his work of such influences as Rilke – and
Eliot and Yeats and (surprisingly) Stephen Spender. His own
voice was already distinctive in its cadences, his ability to
create evocative, arresting images prolific, his way of looking
at things genuinely poetic. Given time, he would have
sloughed off, too, the fashionable accents of the neo-romantic
nineteen-forties. In short, Sidney Keyes remains one of the
most *promising* poets of this century for his achievement was
only limited by his immaturity. Though his work is less
satisfying than that of older poets killed in the war – Keith
Douglas and Alun Lewis – though many of his poems are
flawed with the stage-props of self-indulgent romanticism,
his prophetic lines of personal doom remain viable and his
youthful, elegiac verses of love and death, continue to engage
us now, almost thirty years after they were composed.

TIME WILL NOT GRANT

Time will not grant the unlined page
Completion or the hand respite:
The Magi stray, the heavens rage,
The careful pilgrim stumbles in the night.

Take pen, take eye and etch
Your vision on this unpropitious time;
Faces are fluid, actions never reach
Perfection but in reflex or in rhyme.

Take now, not soon; your lost
Minutes roost home like curses,
Nicolo, Martin, every unhoused ghost
Proclaims time's strange reverses.

Fear was Donne's peace; to him,
Charted between the minstrel cherubim,
Terror was decent. Rilke tenderly
Accepted autumn like a rooted tree.
But I am frightened after every good day
That all my life must change and fall away.

HOPES FOR A LOVER

I'd have you proud as red brocade
And such a sight as Venus made
Extravagantly stepping from a shell.

I'd have you clear your way before
With such a look as Aias wore
On his way back from hell.

I'd have you strong as spider's strand
And all volcanic as the land
Where the nymph fooled that cunning Ulysses.

I'd have you arrogantly ride
Love's flurry, as the turning seas
Bore Arion upon a fish.
My last and dearest wish –
That you should let the arrows of my pride
Come at you again and again and never touch you.

THE PROMISED LANDSCAPE
(For R. -J.)

How shall I sing for you –
Sharing only
The scared dream of a soldier:
A young man's unbearable
Dream of possession?
How shall I sing for you
With the foul tongue of a soldier?

We march through new mountains
Where crows inhabit
The pitiful cairns.
At morning, the rock-pools
Are matted with ice.
But you are the mountains
And you the journey.

We lie in a ruined farm
Where rats perform
Marvels of balance
Among the rafters.
And rain kisses my lips
Because you are the sky
That bends always over me.

How shall I sing for you
Knowing only
The explorer's sorrow,
The soldier's weariness?
New ranges and rivers
Are never quite revealing
Your promised figure.

How dare I sing for you
I the least worthy
Of lovers you've had:
You the most lovely
Of possible landscapes?

THE SNOW

They said, It will be like snow falling –
To-night a hollow wind beating the laurels,
And in the morning quiet, the laurels quiet,
The soft sky resting on the treetops and
The earth not crying any more.

I read it would be safe, like snow lying
Locked in a secret promise with the ground.
And the clear distances, the friendly hills
Would whisper, It is easy, easy as sleep
To the lost traveller frozen in the field.

But now it's come, how different without
Those reassuring voices. Now I face
The bright white glare of January, naked
Among the clashing laurels, while the earth
Stumbles and cries like any lonely lover.

From A GARLAND FOR JOHN CLARE

I'd give you wild flowers for decking
Your memory, those few I know:
Far-sighted catseye that so soon turns blind
And pallid after picking; the elder's curdled flowers,
That wastrel witch-tree; toadflax crouching
Under a wall; and even the unpersistent
Windflowers that wilt to rags within an hour . . .
These for a token. But I'd give you other
More private presents, as those evenings
When under lime-trees of an earlier summer
We'd sing at nine o'clock, small wineglasses
Set out and glittering; and perhaps my friend
Would play on a pipe, competing with the crickets
My lady Greensleeves, fickle as fine weather
Or the lighter-boy who loved a merchant's girl.
Then we would talk, or perhaps silently
Watch the night coming.
Those evenings were yours, John, more than mine.
And I would give you books you never had;
The valley of the Loire under its pinewoods;
My friend Tom Staveley; the carved stone bridge
At Yalding; and perhaps a girl's small face
And hanging hair that are important also.
I'd even give you part in my shared fear:
This personal responsibility
For a whole world's disease that is our nightmare –
You who were never trusted nor obeyed
In anything, and so went mad and died.
We have too much of what you lacked.
Lastly, I'd ask a favour of you, John:

The secret of your singing, of the high
Persons and lovely voices we have lost.
You knew them all. Even despised and digging
Your scant asylum garden, they were with you.
When London's talkers left you, still you'd say
You were the poet, there had only ever been
One poet – Shakespeare, Milton, Byron
And mad John Clare, the single timeless poet.
We have forgotten that. But sometimes I remember
The time that I was Clare, and you unborn.

From SOUR LAND

At Stanton Harcourt in Oxfordshire there is an ancient tower in which Pope completed the fifth book of his *Iliad*, when illness and disillusionment were beginning to oppress him.

So to his perch appropriate with owls
The old lame poet would repair,
When sorrow like a tapeworm in his bowels
Drove him to Troy and other men's despair.

His lame leg twisted on the spiral stair,
He cursed the harsher canker in his heart;
Then in the turret he would scrawl and glare
And long to pull his enemies apart.

When night came knocking at the panes
And bats' thin screeching pierced his head,
He thought of copulation in the lanes
And bit his nails and praised the glorious dead.

At dawn the lapwings cried and he awoke
From dreams of Paris drowned in Helen's hair;
He drew his pride about him like a cloak
To face again the agony of the stair.

From LOVER'S COMPLAINT

The trains cry and are frightened
Far from my distraction; spare
My peace, my voice, my city
Of desolation, desolate because you are there.

There was a month and two people walked in it
But were not you or I:
My sight is broken and the signs are taken
That kept me safe in abject poetry.

Spare too my willing mind
That served your images:
There is a night and two people lie in it,
And the green planet rages.

Were I to pass now on the creaking stair
You would not know my face:
The months and the night and my own mind
Have taken a ghost's grace.

For my private streets and summers
Are any alien comer's;
And the tall miraculous city
That I walked in will never house me.

TO KEEP OFF FEARS

Fear of jammed window and of rising footsteps
Out of fear's stair, where a tall phantom mounts
Through time and action at the brain:

Fear of the enormous mountain leaning
Across thought's lake, where blinded fishes move
As cold and intricate as love:

Fear of the fishermen
Who raised Leviathan
On a steel line from his creative mirror:
Fear of the moonlight shifting against the door:

Fear finally of tripwire and garotte
Reaching possessive from an easy air:
These bring the careful man into despair.

Then let me never crouch against the wall
But meet my fears and fight them till I fall.

THE EXPECTED GUEST

The table is spread, the lamp glitters and sighs;
Light on my eyes, light on the high curved iris
And springing from glaze to steel, from cup to knife
Makes sacramental my poor midnight table,
My broken scraps the pieces of a god.

O when they bore you down, the grinning soldiers,
Was it their white teeth you could not forget?
And when you met the beast in the myrtle wood,
When the spear broke and the blood broke out on
   your side,
What Syrian Veronica above you
Stooped with her flaxen cloth as yet unsigned?
And either way, how could you call your darling
To drink the cup of blood your father filled?

We are dying tonight, you in the aged darkness
And I in the white room my pride has rented.
And either way, we have to die alone.
The laid table stands hard and white as tomorrow.
The lamp sings. The West wind jostles the door.
Though broken the bread, the brain, the brave body
There cannot now be any hope of changing
The leavings to living bone, the bone to bread:
For bladed centuries are drawn between us.
The room is ready, but the guest is dead.

THE WILDERNESS

I

The red rock wilderness
Shall be my dwelling-place.

Where the wind saws at the bluffs
And the pebble falls like thunder
I shall watch the clawed sun
Tear the rocks asunder.

The seven-branched cactus
Will never sweat wine:
My own bleeding feet
Shall furnish the sign.

The rock says 'Endure.'
The wind says 'Pursue.'
The sun says 'I will suck your bones
And afterwards bury you.'

II

Here where the horned skulls mark the limit
Of instinct and intransigeant desire
I beat against the rough-tongued wind
Towards the heart of fire.

So knowing my youth, which was yesterday,
And my pride which shall be gone tomorrow,
I turn my face to the sun, remembering gardens

Planted by others – Longinus, Guillaume de Lorris
And all love's gardeners, in an early May.
O sing, small ancient bird, for I am going
Into the sun's garden, the red rock desert
I have dreamt of and desired more than the lilac's
    promise.
The flowers of the rock shall never fall.

O speak no more of love and death.
And speak no word of sorrow:
My anger's eaten up my pride
And both shall die tomorrow.

Knowing I am no lover, but destroyer,
I am content to face the destroying sun.
There shall be no more journeys, nor the anguish
Of meeting and parting, after the last great parting
From the images of dancing and the gardens
Where the brown bird chokes in its song:
Until that last great meeting among mountains
Where the metal bird sings madly from the fire.

O speak no more of ceremony
Speak no more of fame:
My heart must seek a burning land
To bury its foolish pain.

By the dry river at the desert edge
I regret the speaking rivers I have known;
The sunlight shattered under the dark bridge
And many tongues of rivers in the past.
Rivers and gardens, singing under the willows,
The glowing moon. . . .
                    And all the poets of summer
Must lament another spirit's passing over.

O never weep for me, my love,
Or seek me in this land:
But light a candle for my luck
And bear it in your hand.

III

In this hard garden where the earth's ribs
Lie bare from her first agony, I seek
The home of the gold bird, the predatory Phoenix.
O louder than the tongue of any river
Call the red flames among the shapes of rock:
And this is my calling. . . .
                              Though my love must sit
Alone with her candle in a darkened room
Listening to music that is not present or
Turning a flower in her childish hands
And though we were a thousand miles apart . . .
This is my calling, to seek the red rock desert
And speak for all those who have lost the gardens,
Forgotten the singing, yet dare not find the desert –
To sing the song that rises from the fire.
  It is not profitable to remember
How my friends fell, my heroes turned to squalling
Puppets of history; though I would forget
The way of this one's failure, that one's exile –
How the small foreign girl
Grew crazed with her own beauty; how the poet
Talks to the wall in a deserted city;
How others danced until the Tartar wind
Blew in the doors; or sitting alone at midnight
Heard Solomon Eagle beat his drum in the streets:
This is the time to ask their pardon
For any act of coldness in the past.

There is no kind of space can separate us:
No weather, even this cruel sun, can change us;
No dress, though you in shining satin walk
Or you in velvet, while I run in tatters
Against the fiery wind. There is no loss,
Only the need to forget. This is my calling ...
   But behind me the rattle of stones underfoot,
Stones from the bare ridge rolling and skidding:
A voice I know, but had consigned to silence,
Another calling: my own words coming back. ....

'And I would follow after you
Though it were a thousand mile:
Though you crossed the deserts of the world to the
      kingdom of death, my dear,
I would follow after you and stand beside you there.'

IV

Who is this lady, flirting with the wind,
Blown like a tangle of dried flowers through the desert?
This is my lover whom I left
Alone at evening between the candles –
White fingers nailed with flame – in an empty house.
Here we have come to the last ridge, the river
Crossed and the birds of summer left to silence.
And we go forth, we go forth together
With our lank shadows dogging us, scrambling
Across the raw red stones.
                    There is no parting
From friends, but only from the ways of friendship;
Nor from our lovers, though the forms of love
Change often as the landscape of this journey
To the dark valley where the gold bird burns.

I say, Love is a wilderness and these bones
Proclaim no failure, but the death of youth.
We say, You must be ready for the desert
Even among the orchards starred with blossom,
Even in spring, or at the waking moment
When the man turns to the woman, and both are afraid.
All who would save their life must find the desert –
The lover, the poet, the girl who dreams of Christ,
And the swift runner, crowned with another laurel:
They all must face the sun, the red rock desert,
And see the burning of the metal bird.
Until you have crossed the desert and faced that fire
Love is an evil, a shaking of the hand,
A sick pain draining courage from the heart.

We do not know the end, we cannot tell
That valley's shape, nor whether the white fire
Will blind us instantly. . . .
                              Only we go
Forward, we go forward together, leaving
Nothing except a worn-out way of loving.

V

Flesh is fire, the fire of flesh burns white
Through living limbs: a cold fire in the blood.
We must learn to live without love's food.

We shall see the sky without birds, the wind
Will blow no leaves, will ruffle no new river.
We shall walk in the desert together.
Flesh is fire, frost and fire.
We have turned in time, we shall see

The Phoenix burning under a rich tree.
Flesh is fire.

Solomon Eagle's drum shall be filled with sand:
The dancers shall wear out their skilful feet,
The pretty lady be wrapped in a rough sheet.

We go now, but others must follow:
The rivers are drying, the trees are falling,
The red rock wilderness is calling.

And they will find who linger in the garden
The way of time is not a river but
A pilferer who will not ask their pardon.

Flesh is fire, frost and fire:
Flesh is fire in this wilderness of fire
Which is our dwelling.

DOUGLAS DUNN

DOUGLAS DUNN

IN a recent *Northwest Review* interview, the American critic, Leslie Fiedler, remarked. 'There is no really interesting poetry being written now in Britain by young people, thirty and under ...' During the last three years, though, several young British poets have had first books published which suggest that Leslie Fiedler and those who agree with him, are going to be proved hopelessly wrong.

One such poet is Douglas Dunn who was born in 1942 in Inchinnan on the south bank of the Clyde in Renfrewshire, Scotland. Since the age of seventeen until recently – he is now freelancing – Douglas Dunn has been working in libraries, and it was only in the late sixties that he read English at Hull University. It was while he was a mature student that he lived in a terrace house off Terry Street in Hull and wrote those poems that comprise the first section of his book called *Terry Street* which was published in 1969.

Referring to the actual locality, Terry Street, Douglas Dunn has written in *Poetry Book Society Bulletin No. 62*, 'Terry Street became for me a place of sad sanity. It was an alternative to the gaudy shams everywhere, a cave under a waterfall. But in thinking of Terry Street like this I was probably kidding myself into believing there could be a place not entirely of the age and yet handy enough to it for purposes of observation. Poverty makes men look foolish as well as their lives uncomfortable and I was no exception. I began to feel strange and lost, as though I was trying to inflict loneliness on myself and I came to dislike Terry Street, and left it, although I still live in Hull.'

The Terry Street Douglas Dunn describes, or rather recreates, is as real and as unreal a place as say, Dylan Thomas' *Under Milk Wood*. However, whereas Dylan Thomas created eccentric people with individual names, the characters who live in Mr. Dunn's 'fictional' Terry Street are anonymous, working class, generic figures. They are dustmen and policemen and priests on black bikes; they are young women in rollers 'the type who burst each other's blackheads'; they are old men wearing long underwear and coughing; they are insomniacs who at their night windows make 'small red lights at their mouths'. Above all they are *nameless* and not known. They are shadowy, 'they are part of the silence of places'.

> If you turn your back on it, people are only noises,
> Laughs, footsteps, conversations, hands working.

Wallace Stevens once remarked that 'the imagination loses vitality as it ceases to adhere to what is real'. However fanciful, however much viewed from that cave behind the waterfall, the working class life that Mr. Dunn writes about is never unhinged altogether from the realities of the actual Terry Street in Hull. The working class inhabitants are not glamourized. The taste of the young women is dubious. They 'mix up colours'. Moreoever they are often 'fat and unlovely' and come home after a boozy night out 'supported and kissed and bad-tempered'. Even the old women are caught with their pants down: 'Old women are seen wiping in doorless toilets'.

And yet these people – the women, the old men, the young men on their bicycles, the individuals of Terry Street in their work and in their leisure are not patronized or devalued as human beings. On the contrary, Mr. Dunn's fine achievement is to see what is dignified and potential, even beautiful, in this human ungainliness. The word 'compassion' is a debased word having been used too often and too indiscriminately in innumerable blurbs and reviews of poetry books. It is hard, though, to find any other word as apt to describe Douglas Dunn's two-eyed approach to the inhabitants of Terry Street – his right eye being honestly cold, the left eye moist, though never sentimental. It is quite a feat to celebrate ordinary, everyday, simple actions as he does, for instance, in the poem, 'Men of Terry Street':

> But when you see them, home early from work
> Or at their Sunday leisure, they are too tired
>
> And bored to look long at comfortably.
> It hurts to see their faces, too sad or too jovial.
> They quicken their step at the smell of cooking,
> They hold up their children and sing to them.

Nor are the poems in *Terry Street* merely acute, objective reportage. The feeling in them is too personal for that and is, by the way, tactfully topped up to that level which never embarrasses, is never too blatant. What comes through, also, is a longing, a yearning to communicate with those whom the poet is watching and describing and from whom he is irrevocably separated not merely by a window pane but by taste, culture, and education. Thus the young women in rollers outside, emphasize their differences, and *his* refinement and *his* softness:

> This time they see me at my window, among books
> A specimen under glass, being protected
> And laugh at me watching them.
> They minuet to Mozart playing loudly
> On the afternoon Third. They mock me thus,
> They mime my softness.

In Part II of *Terry Street*, the poems are not rooted in such a unified locale. And, in fact, belong to no particular locality at all. A few have obviously sprung directly from memories of his earlier Scottish background. Two such poems are 'Ships' and 'Landscape with One Figure' and though neither are completely successful both illustrate Douglas Dunn's visual power, his ability to paint a whole texture or to conjure up a feeling and mood of things in one single line:

Waves fall from their small heights on river mud.

Such an evocative and commanding visual summary can, on occasions, be too potent for the poem it inhabits. It is as if, now and then, the poem as a whole cannot afford the single line which is, as it were, living so expensively beyond the poem's means. There are, occasionally also, odd rhythmic effects which may not strike Scottish ears so incongruously as they do mine. But these are small quibbles. A Scotsman, particularly a nationalist, might resent the fact that Mr. Dunn has not written more 'Scottish' poems and would probably question him about this. For some this may be a silly question; yet that it is one that concerns Douglas Dunn himself is suggested by this prose comment he himself has made in *The Poetry Society Bulletin*. 'Yeats wrote in a letter of reply to a young woman who had sent him poems '. . . one should love best what is nearest and most interwoven with one's life'. Although I have only just discovered this beautiful piece of advice . . . it is something that I think I have always known. Yeats was, of course, advising that girl to continue writing about her native Ireland, but with a Scotsman's effrontery and recklessness I choose to be blind to the real significance the advice should have for me. Scotland is what I most want to write about and what I am least able to. The only way I can try to describe the poetry I have written so far, and it is not really for me to do this, is to suggest that I have tried to understand the familiar and the ordinary, and that locality has little to do with this.'

In Part II of *Terry Street* he moves further away from the familiar and ordinary:

> The bed breathes its choir of springs as I move.
> I see her face like a face beneath the water,
> Such is the moonlight of Canada.

This kind of excitement, and touch of mystery, is captured too in such poems as 'A Poem in Praise of the British' and 'A Dream of Random Love' where vigorous risks are taken with success.

The poems written since *Terry Street* own the same virtues that are found in either section of that book. Again risks are taken, and visual summaries reward us:

> There is a boat on the river now, and
> Two young men, one rowing, one reading aloud.
> Their shirt sleeves fill with wind, and from the oar
> Drop scales of perfect river like melting glass.

There is an inclination also to list catalogues of events in the present tense – different things happening simultaneously. The 'I' in the poems, as before, continues to be elusive, a presence which is definite but reticent – to the reader the author remains a shadow figure behind frosted glass, a figure looming behind smoke, or to put it another way 'behind a waterfall'. Sometimes his vision is rooted in place as in 'Backwaters' and is characteristically informed by compassion as in 'Under the Stone'. Certainly these new poems are all recognizably by the same distinctive voice. After reading Douglas Dunn's work surely it is impossible to be gloomy about the prospects and the condition of poetry written in Britain in the 1970s?

———————

Douglas Dunn writes:

My idea of culture is as lost a cause as Jacobitism or the Confederacy. It consists of handsome poets dying splendidly; composers whose beauty is positively menacing, playing their own concertos with almost impertinent displays of emotion to a haughty bourgeoisie; wives who are either rich and beautiful but frail and about to die, or robust bluestockings; and painters, embarrassingly talented, who frighten academicians half to death. Additional clichés can be inserted at will – the playwright from the country, the ploughboy poet, the prolific novelist who also slaves in the Inland Revenue. The best of this culture consists (not in the work, which is magnificent and unpopular) but in the letters the artists send to each other, adding up to a better novel than anything Tolstoy, George Eliot, Flaubert or Proust ever dreamt of. Day after day, I kid myself that the world will be inhabited by these people, that art will be Art; but I probably wouldn't like them if we met. Nostalgia, fantasy – they merge so easily, and both are flaws in the mind. Who, however, can deny that artists have lost the greatness of their styles of life, if not also much of the scale of their individual arts? Or am I making up for my own lack by imagining something that never was?

One of my few beliefs about poetry is that it succeeds by its quality of language. Only the words are real in a poem, and if they are fitting will make the feeling and the meaning of the poem effective. Words, words, words: they must have a contemporary elegance, a unique personality. Some subjects may help a poet find such a language (perhaps only once in his life) but I suspect that the nature of the subject matter is unimportant. It only becomes important if the words are right.

There will also be poets who feel that what they write

about is more important than how they write about it. Occasionally, I think I'm numbered among them. Tension between the literary and the documentary is probably quite marked in my work, especially the poems about Terry Street. In fact, it may even be a 'theme'. I'm on a train that puffs between two stations. One is Romantic Sleep, the other is Social Realism. If I ever get off the train, I don't know what station it will be at.

I like a great deal of the new poetry that I read. Contemporary British poetry is remarkably varied and there are plenty of characters about. It's always important that literary politics should be lively, and this is the case now. Literary gossips are thriving, a good sign that all is well. I don't think it matters much if a lot of the inferior stuff is more popular than it ought to be and getting into Penguins. They'll all die anyway, and so will I; better to err on the side of charity. The best art ignores everybody. It is made for a better world, for Arcadia. In this world it can never be anything other than refreshments for a few on the road to death. Education of large numbers results in widespread bad taste, and so only complicates the essential pattern.

What does annoy me about the current literary situation is the central position criticism has usurped itself into. There has been a palace revolution and the tutors to the Emperor's children have seized the throne. The universities are beating literature to death with paperback criticism, making it information or controversy or enthusy-musy. Interpretation has become more respected and better paid than literature itself: the parasites are healthier than the body they feed on. When today's doomsters put their ears to the ground they don't hear the thundering Hun but hordes of scurrying men with diplomas, racing like mice to a burst bag of grain, 'silently and very fast'.

THE PATRICIANS

In small backyards old men's long underwear
Drips from sagging clotheslines.
The other stuff they take in bundles to the Bendix.

There chatty women slot their coins and joke
About the grey unmentionables absent.
The old men weaken in the steam and scratch at their
   rough chins.

Suppressing coughs and stiffnesses, they pedal bikes
On low gear slowly, in their faces
The effort to be upright, the dignity

That fits inside the smell of aromatic pipes.
Walking their dogs, the padded beats of pocket watches
Muffled under ancient overcoats, silences their hearts.

They live watching each other die, passing each other
In their white scarves, too long known to talk,
Waiting for the inheritance of the oldest, a right to
   power.

The street patricians, they are ignored.
Their anger proves something, their disenchantments
Settle round me like a cold fog.

They are the individualists of our time.
They know no fashions, copy nothing but their minds.
Long ago, they gave up looking in mirrors.

Dying in their sleep, they lie undiscovered.
The howling of their dogs brings the sniffing police,
Their middle-aged children from the new estates.

YOUNG WOMEN IN ROLLERS

Because it's wet, the afternoon is quiet.
Children pacified with sweets inside
Their small houses, stroke travelling cats
From the kingdom of dustbins and warm smells.

Young women come to visit their married friend.
Waiting for their hair to set beneath thin scarves,
They walk about in last year's fashions,
Stockingless, in coats and old shoes.

They look strong, white-legged creatures
With nothing to do but talk of what it is to love
And sing the words softly to the new tunes.
The type who burst each other's blackheads

In the street and look in handbag mirrors
While they walk, not talking of the weather;
Who call across the street they're not wearing knickers,
But blush when they pass you alone.

This time they see me at my window, among books,
A specimen under glass, being protected,
And laugh at me watching them.
They minuet to Mozart playing loudly

On the afternoon Third. They mock me thus,
They mime my softness. A landlord stares.
All he has worked for is being destroyed.
The slum rent-masters are at one with Pop.

The movements they imagine go with minuet
Stay patterned on the air. I can see soot,
It floats. The whiteness of their legs has changed
Into something that floats, become like cloth.

They disappear into the house they came to visit.
Out of the open door rush last year's hits,
The music they listen to, that takes up their time
In houses that are monuments to entertainment.

I want to be touched by them, know their lives,
Dance in my own style, learn something new.
At night, I even dream of ideal communities.
Why do they live where they live, the rich and the poor?

Tonight, when their hair is ready, after tea,
They'll slip through laws and the legs of policemen.
I won't be there, I'll be reading books elsewhere.
There are many worlds, there are many laws.

INCIDENT IN THE SHOP

Not tall, her good looks unstylized,
She wears no stockings, or uses cosmetic.

I sense beneath her blouse
The slow expanse of unheld breasts.

I feel the draughts on her legs,
The nip of cheap detergent on her hands.

Under her bed, forgotten winter bulbs
Die of thirst, in the grip of a wild dust.

Her husband beats her. Old women
Talk of it behind her back, watching her.

She buys the darkest rose I ever saw
And tucks the stem into her plastic belt.

THE WORST OF ALL LOVES

Where do they go, the faces, the people seen
In glances and longed for, who smile back
Wondering where the next kiss is coming from?

They are seen suddenly, from the top decks of buses,
On railway platforms at the tea machine,
When the sleep of travelling makes us look for them.

A whiff of perfume, an eye, a hat, a shoe,
Bring back vague memories of names,
Thingummy, that bloke, what's-her-name.

What great thing have I lost, that faces in a crowd
Should make me look at them for one I know,
What are faces that they must be looked for?

But there's one face, seen only once,
A fragment of a crowd. I know enough of her.
That face makes me dissatisfied with myself.

Those we secretly love, who never know of us,
What happens to them? Only this is known.
They will never meet us suddenly in pleasant rooms.

A DREAM OF RANDOM LOVE

Fond women, walking at the edge of woods,
Waiting for chance lovers, they will not come.

Dressed in long raincoats, with deep pockets,
They turn up their collars at the first rain,

And with long, slow steps walk under a tree.
The grass seed sticks to their wet shoes.

In these woods, I am hunting on a grey horse,
Crossing and recrossing streams after deer.

The one I follow leads me to the forest's end,
Where the daylight presses down the fields

With grey and silver. The mare's breath
Blows back in my face. And women are here,

Some sheltering, and some walking away
Into the high grass, up to their waists in seed,

Wading towards the city, where lines of smoke
Mean there are rooms, and men with empty beds.

Of all these women of an equal, silent beauty,
Does it matter which one I will choose or take?

The one I stop at struggles with her coyness.
Her green eyes shine like water on leaves,

My big, uninterested mare champs grass.
I bend from the saddle and lift her up.

Trees and bushes whip past in the easy gallop,
Water springs off leaves, she presses her cheek on my
  back.

And as the pounding of the hooves fades out,
Riding through the wood, to my cave under the
  waterfall,

I hear myself depart, as though there were two of me.
One is the darkness under trees, one is the light above
  open fields.

A POEM IN PRAISE OF THE BRITISH

The regiments of dumb gunners go to bed early.
The soldiers, sleepy after running up and down
The private British Army meadows,
Clean the daisies off their mammoth boots.
The general goes pink in his bath reading
Lives of the Great Croquet Players.
At Aldershot, beside foot-stamping squares,
Young officers drink tea and touch their toes.

Heavy rain everywhere washes up the bones of British.
Where did all that power come from, the wish
To be inert, but rich and strong, to have too much?
Where does glory come from, and when it's gone
Why are old soldiers sour and the banks empty?
But how sweet is the weakness after Empire
In the garden on a flat, safe country shire,
Watching the beauty of the random, spare, superfluous,

Drifting as if in sleep to the ranks of memorialists
That wait like cabs to take us off down easy street,
To the redcoat armies, and the flags and treaties
In the marvellous archives, preserved like leaves in books.
The archivist wears a sword and clipped moustache.
He files our memories, more precious than light,
To be of easy access to politicians of the Right,
Who now are sleeping, like undertakers on black
    cushions,

Thinking of inflammatory speeches and the adoring mob.
What a time would this be for true decadence!

Walking, new-suited, with trim whiskers, swinging
Our gold-knobbed walking sticks, to the best
    restaurants;
Or riding in closed black carriages to discreet salons,
To meet the women made by art, the fashionably
    beautiful;
Or in the garden, read our sonnets by the pool,
Beside small roses, next week's buttonholes.

In this old country, we are falling asleep, under clouds
That are like wide-brimmed hats. This is just right.
The old pederasts on the Brighton promenade
Fall asleep to dream of summer seductions.
The wind blows their hats away, and they vanish
Into the archives of light, where greatness has gone,
With the dainty tea cup and the black gun,
And dancing dragoons in the fields of heaven.

AFTER THE WAR

The soldiers came, brewed tea in Snoddy's field
Beside the wood from where we watched them pee
In Snoddy's stagnant pond, small boys hidden
In pines and firs. The soldiers stood or sat
Ten minutes in the field, some officers apart
With the select problems of a map. Before,
Soldiers were imagined, we were them, gunfire
In our mouths, most cunning local skirmishers.
Their sudden arrival silenced us. I lay down
On the grass and saw the blue shards of an egg
We'd broken, its warm yolk on the green grass,
And pine cones like little hand grenades.

One burst from an imaginary Browning,
A grenade well thrown by a child's arm,
And all these faces like our fathers' faces
Would fall back bleeding, trucks would burst in flames,
A blood-stained map would float on Snoddy's pond.
Our ambush made the soldiers laugh, and some
Made booming noises from behind real rifles
As we ran among them begging for badges,
Our plimsolls on the fallen may-blossom
Like boots on the faces of dead children.
But one of us had left. I saw him go
Out through the gate, I heard him on the road
Running to his mother's house. They lived alone,
Behind a hedge round an untended garden
Filled with broken toys, abrasive loss;
A swing that creaked, a rusted bicycle.
He went inside just as the convoy passed.

UNDER THE STONE

They sleep out the day in Grimsby, Goole, or Hull,
The sleep of Empire sherry and unspeakable liquors,
And clumsily beg at the Saturday cinema queues
From steady workers and their penny-pinching girlfriends,
The washed and sober, who only want to laugh or
    listen.

These men remind them of the back of their minds.
Splendid barbarians, they form tribes in the slums
Up certain dim streets, the tribes of second-hand,
In empty houses no one wants to buy,
Abandoned rooms the poor have given up.

No one wants to see them, in a grey dawn, walk down
The empty streets, an army of unkempt appointments,
Broken promises, as drab as fog,
Like portents meaning bad harvests, unemployment,
Cavalry in the streets and children shouting 'Bread!
    Bread!'

But they mean nothing, they live under the stone.
They are their own failures and our nightmares
Or longings for squalor, the bad meanings we are.
They like it like that. It makes them happy,
Walking the rubble fields where once houses were.

THE FRIENDSHIP OF YOUNG POETS

There must have been more than just one of us,
But we never met. Each kept in his world of loss
The promise of literary days, the friendship
Of poets, mysterious, that sharing of books
And talking in whispers in crowded bars
Suspicious enough to be taken for love.

We never met. My youth was as private
As the bank at midnight, and in its safety
No talking behind backs, no one alike enough
To be pretentious with and quote lines at.

There is a boat on the river now, and
Two young men, one rowing, one reading aloud.
Their shirt sleeves fill with wind, and from the oars
Drop scales of perfect river like melting glass.

BACKWATERS

They are silent places, dilapidated cities
Obscure to the nation, their names spoken of
In the capital with distinct pejorative overtones.

For some, places mean coming to or going from,
Comedians and singers with suitcases
Packed with signed photographs of themselves;

Business-men in sharp suits, come to buy and sell,
Still seeking their paradise of transactions,
The bottomless market, where the mugs live.

For others, places are sites for existence,
Where the roads slow down and come to a stop
Outside where it's good to be, particular places,

Where the instantly recognized people live,
The buses are a familiar colour and the life is
Utterly civilian.

And for a very few, places are merely the dumps
They end up in, backwaters, silent places,
The cheapest rooms of the cheapest towns.

These darker streets, like the bad days in our lives,
Are where the stutterers hide, the ugly and clubfooted,
The radically nervous who are hurt by crowds.

They love the sunlight at street corners
And the tough young men walking out of it,
And the police patrol. Poverty makes fools of them.

They have done so little they are hardly aware of
   themselves.
Unmissed, pensioned, at the far end of all achievements,
In their kiln-baked rooms, they are permanent.

HERBERT WILLIAMS

HERBERT WILLIAMS

In 1967, Dent published an anthology of poetry called *Welsh Voices*. It was edited by Bryn Griffiths who, in his introduction, spoke of 'a new generation of poets' and of 'a renewed vigour in modern Anglo-Welsh verse.' One of the poets of this new generation was Herbert Williams whose work is still unknown outside Wales.

Herbert Williams was born in 1932 at Aberystwyth where he went to school and grew up. Unlike most contemporary poets he did not study at a university but began work as a journalist instead. In 1954 he married and soon after moved to Cardiff, joining the staff of the *South Wales Echo*. He still works for that paper, still lives in Cardiff, and now has five children. He writes poems when he can and when he needs to, enjoying the ordinary blessings of family life, and like most of us is acutely conscious, as his poems declare, of 'time passing'.

> Now it's dark by eight, and on
> dark days it's dark by seven.
> I'm one more season nearer heaven.
> God, years go fast.

'I'm one more season nearer heaven' may echo Dylan Thomas's 'It was my thirtieth year to heaven', yet generally his poetry owes more to R. S. Thomas than to the 'Rimbaud of Swansea'. For Williams focuses on local and ordinary themes without bardic intensity, and almost invariably uses a conversational rather than a singing tone.

In 1963, another anthologist, Margaret O'Donnell, attempted some definitions of Welsh poets writing in English. She rightly remarked on how the Methodist revival had an effect on the life and language of Wales second only to that of the industrial revolution. 'People became contained in small communities whose life centred around their chapel. Their religious code was puritanically strict and conflicted with the passionate romanticism of the Welsh; but on the other hand, the devotional character of their Bible reading and hymn singing provided an outlet for their Celtic fire. The cultural and spiritual environment was limited and narrow, and this together with a strong sense of democratic equality, a fiery spirit of independence and a life of great material hardship, has given to the Welsh poets who today are writing in English a realism far removed from the vague romanticism often considered synonymous with the Celtic spirit'.

Margaret O'Donnell could hardly in 1963 have been referring to the new generation of poets Bryn Griffiths spoke of and of which Herbert Williams is a fine representative. That generation had not then appeared on the scene. But her remarks now, in retrospect, seem prophetically true. For instance, Herbert Williams's realism is far removed from that same romanticism and his hymn-singing and strict chapel past are reflected in his work.

Nevertheless, Herbert Williams's poetry is not entirely without ornament. Occasionally he takes surprisingly old-fashioned lyrical risks as can be seen in these alliterative lines from 'A Celebration'.

> Between the road and river runs
> A row of rusty railings. And just here
> The ragwort grows. A common weed.
> But such a blaze of beauty that it blooms
> Redemption on the urban blasphemy,
> And justifies itself like Magdalene.

Generally his approach is less obviously 'poetic' than this though he remains always direct and seemingly simple. As John Stuart Williams has remarked, 'Herbert Williams writes with a simplicity that conceals a subtlety of response to his subject.'

In fact Herbert Williams's response is often ambiguous, sometimes ambivalent. Thus in his nostalgia for the old tongue, for the old Welsh ways, for the old chapel life, the sentimental romanticism ever dangerously present in such a backward looking glance is tempered by sour realities. Characteristically Herbert Williams reminds himself that the hymns he heard as a boy were dismal:

> I used to hate the sound of them.
> They made me feel like death.

Again, the small individual shop that he recalls from the old days may be more desirable than the 'soulless supermarket' yet Williams also remembers that the shopkeeper was insufferable: 'I hated him, he was too obsequious by far.'

In short, the loving romantic response usually associated with a nostalgia for the past is in Williams's case intimately mixed with a distaste for the reality that was. Over and over, romantic memories are suddenly pulled up short by Herbert Williams's ever encroaching cynical sense of life as it actually existed. History, like childhood, is almost a legend, the poet seems to say, and all those marvellous Welsh tales resolutely apocryphal. And all this nostalgia for a ghost country, for a Wales that never was, this bitterness about contemporary Welsh life with all its inevitable dilutions, is stated with such a plain diction and in such a neutral tone, that a strange tension is set up and contained. It is this tension resulting from his ambivalence of response and plain diction – 'The Aliens' is a good example – that gives his best poems their life. Moreover, as John Stuart Williams has also pointed out, 'The images which seem so easy and sometimes even obvious, often carry other layers of meaning not apparent at a first hearing.'

This is very true. In his poem 'The Inheritor', for instance, Herbert Williams writes about one of his four sons who had to undergo a heart operation. Here is a real situation portrayed economically and with natural feeling. But the poem is so directed that the heart operation finally comes to have a symbolic quality and the poem which began as a personal outcry thus ends as a universal statement.

I do not want to claim too much for Herbert Williams. He is not, despite his satiric attitudes, his fullness of feeling, his nostalgic pessimism, his cynical humour, his anti-heroic stance, a Welsh Philip Larkin. He is linguistically too un-tutored and, sometimes, poems he publishes in the Welsh magazines remain *needlessly* flawed. Even an interesting poem like 'Ghost Country' contains clichés that a more sophisticated poet (who may have less talent) would have avoided. Lines, for instance, like: 'We are children of defeat. And yet our hearts keep faith.'

Nevertheless I like 'Ghost Country' in spite of its flaws and I have included it here along with others I admire more. At his best, Herbert Williams deserves a larger audience than parochial Welsh magazines allow for he has written genuine poems which all of us should be grateful for.

Herbert Williams writes:

I was quite a prolific poet at the age of ten or eleven, when I produced some pre-adolescent love lyrics, very chaste and romantic, but then the affair broke up and I like to think I retired into my shell to avoid any more hurt. Or maybe it was simply that I discovered football. Anyway, I didn't write any more poetry for a long time, and then I scratched around a bit, not sure if I wanted to be like Eliot, Housman or Dylan Thomas, and by the time I produced anything remotely resembling poetry I had reached the ripe old age of 28. The resemblance, I trust, is less remote now, but others might disagree.

At that time I wrote several poems based on characters I had known when growing up in Aberystwyth, a seaside town in West Wales where everyone knows everyone else and they all go for walks on the prom on Sunday afternoon. Jones the Grocer was one of these, and The Old Tongue and The Castle Choir were also inspired (if that's the right word) by my Aberystwyth background. In poems like this there is, I suppose, a sense of loss, but curiously, when living in Aberystwyth I never felt it. My father spoke Welsh, but as my mother didn't we took it for granted that ours was an English-speaking home. It was only when I moved to Cardiff that I was able to see the whole thing in perspective, and it was then that I began to be aware of my lost heritage, if that isn't too pompous a phrase. The heritage was, simply, the Welsh language, and the life which was lived through it: thus The Old Tongue. I suppose I have an ambivalent attitude to the Welsh language, and to Wales itself: not exactly love-hate, for I never hate either, but the love is complex and compounded sometimes of a hellish mixture of desperation and sheer addiction. Wales is a kind of opium for many non-Welsh-speaking Welshmen. We say we long to be free of it, but we are hopelessly enslaved, and we don't really want to be free of it, not at heart. To insist that we are not English is not to be narrowly parochial, nor simply theatrical, nor plain cussed: it's a statement of fact.

The poem Ghost Country deals with what one might call the condition of Wales, for I have been influenced by nationalism to the extent that it has made me aware of the political absorption of Wales into England in the 13th century. But I am not a political animal, still less a political poet. Propagandist poetry bores me, and is probably a contradiction in terms anyway, and it seems to me that some writers in Wales are more concerned with writing poetry for 'the cause' than with simply writing poetry.

One can't, which means I can't, write about Wales all the time. We have our more personal concerns: our families, and the domestic crises which overwhelm us from time to time. (The Inheritor was written a few hours after my eldest son had had a heart operation. I was staying the night at the hospital, and would have said I wasn't in the mood for poetry if the thing hadn't started shaping itself in my head.)

People say my verse is easily understood, and I don't think that's always meant as a compliment. But, for myself, I don't see the virtue in poetry which is written in so private a language that one needs an interpreter. At least, it could have a virtue for oneself, but surely that sort of thing should be kept *to* oneself. There's nothing wrong in asking the reader to make an effort, so long as it's not an impossible effort. Still, since I find it hard to write obscurely this could simply be self-justification.

I have been writing poetry only about ten years, which isn't long really, and as a late starter I like to think my work is still developing. I believe my poetry is taking new directions, and I certainly wouldn't like to be officiously pigeon-holed as an 'Anglo-Welsh' poet. To be purely, if not simply, a poet is surely enough.

THE OLD TONGUE

We have lost the old tongue, and with it
The old ways too. To my father's
Parents it was one
With the *gymanfa ganu*, the rough
Shouts of seafarers, and the slow
Dawn of the universal light.
It was one with the home-made bread, the smell
Of cakes at missionary teas,
And the shadows falling
Remotely on the unattempted hills.

It is all lost, the tongue and the trade
In optimism. We have seen
Gethsemane in Swansea, marked
The massacre of innocents. The dawn
Was false and we invoke
A brotherhood of universal fear.
And the harbour makes
A doldrum of the summer afternoon.

Even the hills are diminished.
They are a gallon of petrol,
There and back. The old salts
Rot. And the bread
Is tasteless as a balance sheet.

Oh yes, there have been gains.
I merely state

That the language, for us,
Is part of the old, abandoned ways.

And when I hear it, regret
Disturbs me like a requiem.

THE CASTLE CHOIR

'And now, *Caersalem*.' Fingers gloved
Against the itch of love flick through
The hymnbooks. Throats are cleared. And then
The harmonies surge out across the bay.
It is the Castle Choir, replete
With righteousness and love of minor keys.
They sing here every Sunday in the summer,
And the tourists stop, their fancy
Tickled by the natives' curious ways.

I used to hate the sound of them.
They made me feel like death. Those hymns,
Admonishing the hedonistic prom.
So we hurried past, derisive
Boyos with an eye for grosser curves
Than those the educated baton traced.

They crucified the sun, those dismal hymns,
And yet they had a relevance.
It wasn't long ago, but then the Welsh
Still had a Sunday. Now
The beaches are transistorized, and joy
Is straining on a less attentive leash.

And Pantycelyn's proud reproaches sound
Like distant music in our alien ears.

DAUGHTER OF THE HOUSE

It is not love that keeps her here, tending
The stubborn enterprise of age. Her hands
Are clinical expressions of a heart
Made bleak by sacrifice, her eyes
Neutralize her therapeutic smile.

Love is an easy master, but her guile
Springs from more terrible demands.
It is the blood's dictatorship, bending
Her uninvited kinship to the part,
Masking indifference with a knack of lies.

JONES THE GROCER

Jones the Grocer, we called him –
A pale man, skilled in servility,
His hands white and soft as the lard he stacked
In small, meticulous rows, his head
Polished and somehow apologetic, as if
He was crowned forever with dishonour.

I hated him, he was too obsequious by far,
Embellishing transactions with fulsome flattery
Of your habits, your appearance, your miserable opinions.
He seemed to exist in a fog
Of self-effacement, through which one caught
The rarest glimpse of a human dignity.

Yet one could suffer the arid washing of his hands
For the joy of that shop, its curiosities,
Like the corner where it was always dusk
And equatorial, aromatic with coffee beans,
And the calendars derisive of topicality,
And the adverts twenty years out of date.

One could suffer it, and gladly suffer it again
To be delivered of this, its successor –
A supermarket, slick and soulless,
Arrogantly accepting the shoppers' homage.

A CELEBRATION

You will know it, the ragwort,
Though not perhaps by name –
A yellow flower, full
Of mischief for the gardener.
A common weed, populous
As common people, and as apt
To make the best of an indifferent lot.
You will know its pertinacious ways,
Its bland possession of a tumbled soil,
And you will wonder why
I celebrate its impudence.

Well, I will tell you. There is a spot
In Cardiff where the Taff
Flows between grubby banks. The view
Is nonexistent. Concrete, bricks,
And traffic brash as pain.
Between the road and river runs
A row of rusty railings. And just here
The ragwort grows. A common weed.
But such a blaze of beauty that it blooms
Redemption on the urban blasphemy,
And justifies itself like Magdalene.

THE ALIENS

They brought a foreign warmth
To valleys bleak with strife
And Calvinism, brewing
A relaxation in the coffee cups.
And sunny voices learned
The mysteries of a tongue
Dark with the shadows of an ancient war.
They read the native ways
But kept, perhaps, an irony
Hidden behind their friendly, Latin eyes.
But they were too polite
To mock our self-denial,
And anyway, it wasn't good for business.

Their cafés, innocent
Of obvious sin, were yet
Viewed with disapproval by the folk
Who idolized a God
Who never smiled on Sunday,
And thunderously visited a curse
On all who stepped inside
To buy a box of matches for
A pipe of surreptitious Sabbath peace.
And yet the cafés spread.
And they became accepted.
And God, at last, was able to relax.

Times change. Some chapels now
Are turned to supermarkets,
The gospel is according to demand.

And hedonistic clubs
Have striptease on a Sunday,
Behind the seventh veil lies the promised land.
But still the Rabaiottis,
Bracchis and Antoniazzis
Keep their faith in God intact
And their attitude polite:
The customer, of course, is always right.

THE ALLIANCE

There will be a measure of sorrow.
And they will come, wearing their
Bereavement on their sleeve.
And they will make the necessary sounds,
And they will take the necessary way
To some utilitarian place where death
Makes every day a territorial gain.
And there they'll watch me decorously put away,
And turn for home, thinking of tea.

And as they eat the funerary bread,
And lubricate their morbid fellowship,
The old familiar courtesies will lull
Their quisling souls to rest. And they will ease
A resignation slyly into place,
And make a prudent settlement with death.

Only my very dear ones, fiercely alone,
Will keep alliance with me. They will blind
Themselves to acquiescence, they will hear
My silence like a terror in the house.

And when the mourners leave, the emptiness
Will be my posthumous identity.

GHOST COUNTRY

Now the weather turns
Accomplice with the landscape. Skies
Become like tracts of fundamentalists,
Livid with threat, hiding the truthful sun,
And pale, enduring grasses bend
Before the wind. The sheep are part
Of nature's language, the remorseless
Dialogue of cumulus and bone.
They stand, grey syllables within
The mountain's grammar. This is no
Limpid pastoral. It speaks
Of refuge from invader, clash
Of sword and culture. Here
We feel as prodigals come home,
Yet strangely changed. Our speech
Is evidence of conquest. We
Are children of defeat. And yet
Our hearts keep faith. This land
Is ours, and in the tongue's
Music, falling on our wayward ears
Like half-remembered songs, we hear
Ourselves, not as we are,
But as we would have been
If English kings
Had kept their distance.
                              White
As winding sheet the snow, and cold
As death the rain. We feel
The chill too late, long
Centuries too late. The land

That would have been is not,
And never will be. Those who yearn
For late amend can not return
To the beleagured halls
Cynddylan knew, nor walk
The ways of Taliesin. They can not
Cheat time and say,
'Now we relive the day
Llewelyn died, and see
No murder at the ford. The year's
Twelve eighty-two, and we
Go on from here.' The stern
Centuries have fled,
And with them all the acts
That would have been accomplished, all the words
We never heard and all the books
That stayed unwritten. They are gone,
The giants of a state that never was,
The princes and the judges, the immense
Gallery of national acclaim,
Philosophers and statemen, they are gone.
Their names are written in the wind that bends
The pale, enduring grasses, and the skies
Are their memorial. Those who burn
To change direction may create
An independent state. It will not be
The Wales that would have been. That land
Is mystery.
               But ghosts
Of our aborted history haunt bays
Where Brummies play and glide
Like mute hosannahs through the countryside.

GENESIS

You are complete again with child.
Your breasts are round and ripe, your body
Swells. Now you are no mere wife, but something
More: a mill of life,
Abundance at your core.

You are still you, and yet you are
Another one besides. Within
Your womb the future grows, and though we'll know
Only the years we live, the rest
Is altered by our love.

Not only son or daughter, but
Their sons and daughters too, and all
The generations who will tell their worth
Till earth runs out of time are now
Awakened by this birth.

Nothing will be the same. Come near,
My love, and let me hear
The heartbeat of a hundred aeons hence
Within your present tense, and bless
Your fruitfulness.

THE INHERITOR

It has come to this
A boy in a bed
Trailing tubes
Fighting for life

It has come to this
The midnight trysts
When Arthur ruled
Generations of love
Have come to this
A boy in a bed
With a modified heart
Good for life
If he lasts this night

It has come to this
The skill of men
With surgical truths
At their fingertips
It has come to this
The primitive zeal
Of men who crouched
In fetid caves
And cheated night
With their fiery craft
It has come to this
The march of man.

It has come to this
A boy in a bed.
My son, my son,
Inheritor.

Selected Bibliography

EDWARD THOMAS:

Collected Poems, Selwyn and Blount Ltd., London, 1920.

Collected Poems, edited with an appreciation by Walter de la Mare, 1928 and reprinted by Faber, London, 1936.

The Prose of Edward Thomas, selected by Roland Gant, The Falcon Press, London, 1948.

New Bearings in English Poetry, F. R. Leavis, Chatto & Windus, London, 1932.

As it Was and *World Without End*, Helen Thomas, Heinemann, London, 1935.

Edward Thomas, Henry Coombes, Chatto & Windus, London, 1956.

Edward Thomas: The Last Four Years, Eleanor Farjeon, London, 1958.

Edward Thomas, Vernon Scannell, Longmans, Green, London, 1963.

Letters from Edward Thomas to Gordon Bottomley, ed. and introduced by R. George Thomas, O.U.P., London, 1968.

Edward Thomas: a critical biography, W. Cooke, Faber, London, 1970.

The Writings of E. Thomas, Jeremy Hooker, The Anglo-Welsh Review, 1970.

A Ghostly Harvest, Dan Jacobson, The Review, No. 22, 1970.

TED HUGHES:

The Hawk in the Rain, Faber, London, 1957.

Lupercal, Faber, London, 1960.

Wodwo, Faber, London, 1967.

Poetry in the Making, Faber, London, 1967.

Crow, Faber, London, 1970.

Kinds of Poetry, Edwin Muir, New Statesman, September 28th, 1957.

Ted Hughes, A. E. Dyson, The Critical Quarterly, Autumn, 1959.

A Vision of Reality, Frederick Grubb, Chatto & Windus, London, 1965.

The New Poets, M. L. Rosenthal, Oxford University Press, New York, 1967.

The Poetry of Ted Hughes, Daniel Hoffman, Shenandoah, Virginia, 1968.

Modern Writers, H. G. Earnshaw, W. & R. Chambers, Edinburgh & London, 1968.

The Survival of Poetry, Ed. Martin Dodsworth, Faber, London, 1970.

Contemporary Poets of the English Language, St. James Press, Chicago and London, 1970.

SIDNEY KEYES:

The Iron Laurel, Routledge, London, 1942.

The Cruel Solstice, Routledge, London, 1944.

Collected Poems, with a memoir by Michael Meyer, Routledge, London, 1945.

Minos of Crete, ed. Michael Meyer, Routledge, London, 1948.

Poets of 1939–45 War, R. N. Currey, Longmans, Green, London.

Sidney Keyes: a biographical enquiry, John Guenther, London Magazine, Editions, 1967.

Thoughts on the Forties, Derek Stanford, Poetry Review, Autumn, 1969.

DAVID WRIGHT:

Moral Stories, Verschoyle, London, 1954.

Monologue of a Deaf Man, André Deutsch, London, 1958.

Adam at Evening, Hodder and Stoughton, London, 1965.

Nerve Ends, Hodder and Stoughton, London, 1969.

Deafness: A Personal Account, Allen Lane, London, 1969.

David Wright: An Impression, Derek Stanford, Poetry Quarterly, Summer, 1951.

DAVID WRIGHT: – *contd.*

    The Mid-Century English Poetry, ed. with introduction by David Wright, Penguin Books, 1965.

    Contemporary Poets of the English Language, St. James Press, Chicago and London, 1970.

DOUGLAS DUNN:

    Poetry Introduction No. 1, Faber, London, 1969.

    Terry Street, Faber, London, 1969.

    Backwaters, Supplement of The Review, No. 25, 1971.

Poetry Book Society Bulletin No. 62, London, 1969.

Book Review – Anthony Thwaite, New Statesman, October 3rd, 1969.

Book Review – M. Dodsworth, The Listener, December 11th, 1969.

Poetry of 1969, T.L.S. 8, Oxford University Press, London, 1970.

HERBERT WILLIAMS:

    The Dinosaurs, introduced by John Stuart Williams, A Poetry Wales pamphlet, Triskel Press, Cardiff, 1966.

    The Trophy, Christopher Davies Ltd. Llandybie, Carmarthenshire, Wales, 1967.

Book Review – Sally Roberts, Poetry Wales, Summer, 1967.

Book Review – Charles Elliott, The Anglo-Welsh Review, Winter, 1967.

The Second Flowering, Meic Stephens, Poetry Wales, Winter, 1967.